Tastefully Small

Savory Bites

EASY, SOPHISTICATED HORS D'OEUVRES FOR
EVERY OCCASION

KIM HENDRICKSON

Published by Salvia Press. • 45 South Pearl Street • Pearl River, New York 10965 • 845-633-3961

Web site: www.salviapress.com • info@salviapress.com • SAN Number: 859-3914

Library of Congress Cataloging-in-Publication Data

Hendrickson, Kim, 1954–

  Tastefully small savory bites : easy, sophisticated hors d'oeuvres for any occasion / by Kim Hendrickson.

    p. cm.

  Includes bibliographical references and index.

  ISBN-13: 978-0-9844315-0-2 (alk. paper)

  ISBN-10: 0-9844315-0-0 (alk. paper)

  1. Appetizers. I. Title.

  TX740.H4676 2010

  641.8´12—dc22   2009040963

PHOTOGRAPHS: Tricia Solyn (Dishware by Revol; see Resources)

ILLUSTRATIONS: Leslie Kruzicki

COVER DESIGN AND LAYOUT: Meg Buchner

                Catherine Rawson and Brett Rand Guldemond (Rand & Rawson Studios)

FOOD STYLING: Alan Muskat

Printed in China

For Patty, my W.G.G. partner and lifelong friend

"Hors d'oeuvres have always been a pathetic interest for me:
they remind me of one's childhood that one goes through,
wondering what the next course is going to be like—
and during the rest of the menu one wishes one
had eaten more of the hors d'oeuvres."

Saki (H. H. Munro)

Caramelized Onion Lamb Cups (page 38)

Acknowledgments

I could not have accomplished this volume without the help of a group of very talented people:

Doug Brown, publisher of Atlantic Publishing, for without his support, this series would never have seen the light of day.

Nancy Miller, who painstakingly makes me look not just good but great on paper. Her detailed corrections have made this book presentable while teaching me many editing and proofing tips. Now, if I can just remember them!

Patty Logan, who has supported me with kindness and encouragement throughout this project as well as throughout my life.

Mary Ellen, my former high school English teacher, for so carefully proofing this manuscript before it went to press.

Tricia Solyn, who has once again made the photos look glamorous and mouthwatering. Her photographic skill, flexibility, and good-humored patience made it possible to take all these photos in a short amount of time.

Leslie Kruzicki, for her detailed watercolors, which add so much style to this series, not to mention her patience in dealing with my own less than perfect photographs!

Alan Muskat, whose creative suggestions and prodding all along the way make this book—and me—better each time we interact. Alan worked closely with Tricia in setting up the photos and has managed many other details that support this project and me in so many ways. He always believes in me, even when I forget to!

Meg Buchner, for this series's distinctive layout. Her patience is boundless and Lord knows I need it.

Writing a book is just the beginning of a long process, and without the support of distributors who make it possible for small stores to buy books like mine, few would ever get sold. I want to thank Ron of Harold Imports and Bruce of Benjamin Books for their support of my books and of me as an author.

Scallion Puff Pillows (page 110)

Introduction

What is it about hors d'oeuvres that so many people like so much? For me, small bites of powerful flavor, savory or not, excite and satisfy my Gemini palate. A variety of small bites sends me into a dog wiggle of delight, while a large plate of food leaves me bored (and I like to eat!). The variety in a number of small appetizers makes me so satisfied that I'm full and happy before I need to order an entrée. And I know I'm not the only one…

Appetizers include everything from soup and salad to anything that starts a meal, but my heart goes out for little packages. Flavor isn't the only reason I prefer small bites; the aesthetics are appealing, too. Like beautiful chocolates or creative cookies in a showcase, the variety, colors, and diversity of textures and smells make me happy down to my toes.

The recipes in this book contain flavor combinations that I love, in shapes and presentations that will delight your guests yet can be made without anxiety or difficulty. Whether with drinks before dinner, an afternoon tea, or a sumptuous buffet, these recipes will wow your guests and leave you with energy to enjoy the party. These recipes are easy—and very far from the same old variations on meatballs and marinated shrimp. I'm pleased to give you the tools and inspiration to make your next gathering a tastefully small, unique experience. Let me know how it goes…

Contents

Meat Bites

Poultry and Egg Bites

Vegetable Bites

Pastry-Based Bites

Naked Canapés

Helpful Tips

Tart Pink Scallops (page 18)

Seafood Bites

Over the years I've noticed that people at buffets and cocktail parties pay the most attention to hors d'oeuvres made with shellfish. Phrases like "I want to hold out for the shrimp" are heard frequently. So, when assembling an assortment of hors d'oeuvres, don't forget seafood bites, especially the shrimp. You may want to not serve them all at once, because they will disappear!

This chapter offers a variety of seafood bites, focusing on favorite seafoods that are a delight to the eye and easy to prepare.

- Mini Crab Cheesecakes
- Lobster Salad Cubes
- Tart Pink Scallops
- Fruited Jumbo Shrimp
- Thai Shrimp Baskets
- Curried Cream Mussels
- Sea Bass with Minted Pea Purée
- Squid Ceviche
- Persimmon Shrimp Bruschetta

Mini Crab Cheesecakes

These little cakes are based on a large cheesecake I've been serving at parties for years. It has never disappointed my guests and is easy to make in advance. However, I've always been frustrated by how sloppy it looks after it has been cut into. Making mini versions of this cake eliminates the problem, and the crab garnish intensifies the flavor. Small is beautiful, isn't it?

Yield: 32 cheesecakes

1 cup fresh bread crumbs

½ cup grated Parmesan cheese

4 tablespoons (½ stick) unsalted butter, melted

1 tablespoon extra-virgin olive oil

1 cup finely chopped onion

1 cup finely chopped red bell pepper

1 cup chopped assorted mushrooms

28 ounces cream cheese, softened

2 teaspoons salt

1 teaspoon freshly ground pepper

4 eggs

½ cup heavy cream

10 ounces crabmeat, drained and picked over (about 2 cups)

1 cup grated Gouda cheese (about 4 ounces)

½ cup chopped fresh parsley

1 cup crabmeat, drained and picked over, as garnish

2 mini cheesecake pans—1¾ × 2-inch cup size
(or 2 regular muffin pans)

Photo: page 76

Preheat oven to 350°F. Combine bread crumbs, Parmesan, and melted butter in a small bowl. Spoon 1 tablespoon into each cup and press down to flatten. Bake until bottoms are golden brown, about 8 minutes, and set aside, leaving oven on.

Heat oil in a skillet over medium-high heat. Add onion and bell pepper and sauté for 2 minutes. Add mushrooms and sauté until liquid has evaporated and the mushrooms begin to brown.

Using an electric mixer, beat cream cheese, salt, and pepper in a large bowl until fluffy. Beat in eggs 1 at a time, then heavy cream. Gently stir in cooled vegetables, crabmeat, Gouda, and parsley.

Spoon about ¼ cup filling into each cup. Bake in the center of the oven until they puff up and brown, about 25 minutes. Cool. Can be prepared a day ahead and refrigerated.

Release cakes from pans and place in muffin papers for easy handling. Garnish with remaining crabmeat and bring to room temperature before serving.

Modify

Replace the crab with tiny whole shrimp. Omit the Gouda and mushrooms but add chopped spinach and ½ cup cocktail sauce for a change of pace.

Magnify

This recipe can easily be baked in a 9- or 10-inch springform pan for 1½ hours. Refrigerate to make serving easier. Tomato roses with parsley make a lovely garnish in the center of this grand savory cake.

Lobster Salad Cubes

A visit to Rhode Island this past year reminded me of why simple, fresh ingredients make all the difference. Lobster salad, to me, was always an expensive and flavorless experience until this visit. Friends made a local favorite, lobster rolls, for a party buffet, and as I was filling the rolls before the party, I found every other spoonful ended up in my mouth! These stuffed cubes are my attempt to put the focus on the salad without too much bread getting in the way.

Yield: 32 cubes

¼ cup mayonnaise

4 teaspoons minced green scallions

4 teaspoons minced fresh parsley

2 teaspoons finely grated lemon zest

2 teaspoons fresh lemon juice

2 cups chopped, cooked lobster meat

Salt and freshly ground pepper

1 loaf white bread, unsliced, with crust removed

Vegetable oil for brushing

Curly parsley, as garnish

Whisk together mayonnaise, scallions, parsley, lemon zest, and juice in a medium bowl. Fold in lobster meat. Season with salt and pepper to taste. Refrigerate until ready to fill and serve.

Preheat oven to 350°F. Trim the loaf into a 3 × 3 × 12-inch block. Cut the loaf lengthwise in half, and then each half in half so that you end up with 4 loaves, each 1½ inches square in cross section and 12 inches long. Cut these loaves into 8 equal 1½-inch cubes. Take a small paring knife and cut a well about halfway down into each cube and about ¾ inch across.

Using a small pastry brush, brush cubes lightly with oil. Place on an unlined baking sheet and bake until bread is toasted, about 10 minutes. Cool. These bread cubes can be prepared in advance and stored in an airtight container in a cool place for 3 to 4 days.

Mound a spoonful of lobster salad into each cube and garnish with a parsley leaf. Filled cubes may be refrigerated in a sealed container for up to 4 hours before serving.

Modify

Replace cubes with mini cream puffs, and add ½ cup finely minced parsley added to the lobster mixture.

Magnify

Cut sheets of puff pastry into 2 × 3-inch rectangles and bake until golden. Spread pastry with lobster salad, add another piece, then more lobster, and one more pastry on top. Center on an appetizer plate and sprinkle a border of chopped parsley, red or orange bell pepper finely chopped, and grated lemon zest for a classy meal starter. Serves 6.

Tart Pink Scallops

When I'm baking, I usually know before a new recipe is completed that I'll love it because I start eating the ingredients before the dish is finished. While photographing this recipe, I couldn't stop eating the extra scallops waiting in the kitchen as "stand-ins." The pink grapefruit is so pretty against the golden scallops, and the tart citrus is a perfect contrast to the sweet seafood and crisp cucumber.

Yield: 24 bites

2 red or pink grapefruits

2 tablespoons honey or agave syrup*

2 tablespoons fresh lemon juice

½-inch piece peeled fresh ginger

12 sea scallops (about 1 pound), halved horizontally

¼ teaspoon salt

Freshly ground pepper

¼ cup extra-virgin olive oil

1 large English cucumber

1 cup alfalfa sprouts, as garnish

Photo: page 12

Peel each grapefruit, removing all the white pith. Using a sharp paring knife, carve out sections between membranes while holding fruit over a bowl to catch the juice. Squeeze membranes to remove all of the juice. Set grapefruit sections aside.

Strain juice into a small saucepan and place over high heat. Add honey, lemon juice, and ginger. Boil, stirring occasionally, until sauce becomes syrupy, is reduced by half, and takes on an amber color, about 4 minutes. Remove from heat and cool completely. Discard ginger.

Season scallops with salt and pepper. Heat 2 tablespoons of the oil in a skillet over medium heat. Add half the scallops and cook, undisturbed, until they are browned on the bottom, about 4 minutes. Turn scallops over and cook for another 30 seconds. Repeat with remaining oil and scallops.

Slice unpeeled cucumber into ¼-inch rounds. Place 1 scallop half on top of each cucumber slice, browned side up. Spoon on a little grapefruit syrup, top with a piece or two of grapefruit, and drizzle with a bit more syrup. If grapefruit sections are too large, cut them in half so the grapefruit fits attractively on top. Top with a few sprouts and serve at room temperature. These can be assembled up to 2 hours ahead and kept in the refrigerator before serving.

*Agave is a natural sweetener found in most natural foods stores.

Modify

Replace scallops with 24 large cooked shrimp and grapefruit with 1½ cups pitted, halved fresh cherries and 1 cup unsweetened cherry juice.

Magnify

Turn this into a refreshing salad. Do not reduce the liquids to a syrup; instead, add 2 tablespoons olive oil to the grapefruit and lemon juices and honey along with 1 teaspoon grated ginger and stir to create a quick dressing. Place some salad greens on a small plate, top with grapefruit sections, then some scallops, and sprinkle the sprouts and dressing over the plate. Serves 4.

Fruited Jumbo Shrimp

When I was in high school, I tried out a new recipe for a picnic. The recipe called for chicken, shrimp, red pepper, and cantaloupe. It was the first time I had ever tasted the pairing of meat and shellfish with fruit—my mom was a very plain cook! I loved that salad and prepared it many, many times afterward. I've never lost my taste for fruit and seafood, especially shrimp.

Yield: 24 shrimp

¼ cup fresh lemon juice

2 bay leaves

2 teaspoons salt

1 teaspoon whole black peppercorns

24 shrimp, jumbo or extra-large, deveined and, peeled but with tails left on

¾ cup peeled, finely chopped mango

½ cup peeled, seeded, finely chopped cantaloupe

¼ cup pomegranate seeds

¼ cup peeled, seeded, finely chopped cucumber

1 small serrano chile, seeded and, finely chopped

2 teaspoons rice vinegar

1 tablespoon chopped fresh cilantro

Photo: page 25

Bring 6 cups water, lemon juice, bay leaves, salt, and peppercorns to a boil in a medium saucepan, over medium heat. Add shrimp and cook just until they turn pink, about 2 minutes. Drain shrimp and set aside.

Combine mango, cantaloupe, pomegranate seeds, cucumber, chile, vinegar, and cilantro in a small bowl. Place in a small sieve over a bowl until ready to use.

Using a sharp paring knife, cut a partial slice through the ridge on the shrimp where the vein was located: not to separate, but enough to fold open or "butterfly" shrimp so it can stand securely with its tail dramatically in the air. Spoon fruit salsa into the depression just under the curved tail. Serve chilled or at room temperature.

Modify

Replace pomegranate seeds with chopped strawberries and cucumber with chopped jicama.

Magnify

Cook shrimp as directed and chop into ½-inch pieces. Add 1 cup each diced mango, apple, pineapple, and cucumber. Toss all fruit and shrimp together. Drizzle with a dressing made with ¼ cup rice vinegar, 2 tablespoons extra-virgin olive oil, 2 tablespoons chopped cilantro, and 1 finely chopped serrano chile with seeds removed. Serve in Bibb lettuce cups as a cold appetizer or light lunch. Serves 4.

Thai Shrimp Baskets

The flavors of pad Thai are a delight to me, but my least favorite part is the noodles. For this small bite, I've upped the egg, dropped the noodles, and kept that classic sweet and spicy flavor. Everything can be prepared in advance, so all you have to do is assemble before serving.

Yield: 24 baskets

Wonton wrappers

1 tablespoon tamarind paste*

¼ cup boiling water

2 tablespoons fish sauce*

1 tablespoon rice vinegar

2 tablespoons sugar

½ teaspoon cayenne pepper

¼ cup vegetable oil

1 cup chopped raw shrimp (about 10 large shrimp)

½ teaspoon salt

1 egg

2 cloves garlic, forced through a garlic press

1 small shallot, minced

1 cup shredded mixed vegetables (carrot, cauliflower, eggplant, zucchini)

2 tablespoons chopped fresh cilantro

½ lemon

¼ cup finely chopped unsalted peanuts

1 scallion, finely chopped, green part only

¼ cup peanut halves, as garnish

Cilantro leaves, as garnish

Miniature muffin pan

Preheat oven to 350°F. Trim wonton wrappers (cut off corners) so that each can be pressed into and just overlap the edges of each ungreased muffin cup. Bake for 5 to 8 minutes or just until edges are browned. Remember that exposed edges burn easily. These cups can be prepared up to a week in advance if stored in a cool, airtight container.

Combine tamarind and boiling water in a small bowl and stir until paste is dissolved. Add fish sauce, rice vinegar, sugar, cayenne, and 2 tablespoons of the oil. Stir to combine and set aside.

Heat 1 tablespoon of the oil in a small skillet, over medium-high heat. Add shrimp, season with ¼ teaspoon salt and cook until browned, about 2 minutes. Place in a bowl.

Continued on next page

*Tamarind paste and fish sauce can be found in specialty stores; otherwise use ¼ cup each lime juice and water.

Modify

Exchange the egg and/or shrimp for chicken pieces or beef strips, or use different vegetables. It is the tamarind paste that flavors any change successfully.

Magnify

Toss filling with cooked rice noodles or very thin spaghetti for a good and easy appetizer or main dish.

Whisk egg with ¼ teaspoon salt in a small bowl. Add to skillet over medium-high heat and scramble just until egg is barely set and still quite runny. Add to shrimp.

Add remaining 1 tablespoon oil to the skillet over medium-high heat. Just as oil begins to smoke, add garlic and shallot and stir-fry until just browned, about 1½ minutes. Add shredded vegetables and cilantro and continue to cook until vegetables are barely tender, 2 to 3 minutes. Add reserved egg, shrimp, and tamarind-vinegar sauce and increase heat to high. Vigorously scramble with a wooden spatula so all of the ingredients get warmed and egg cooks and browns, 1 to 2 minutes longer. Squeeze lemon juice over the filling, then add chopped peanuts and scallion and toss.

Spoon filling into wonton cups and garnish with peanut halves and cilantro leaves.

Fruited Jumbo Shrimp (page 20)

Curried Cream Mussels

When teaching, I don't know how many times I've heard students say they either love or hate the flavor of curry. I guess with some flavors there is no middle ground, but this recipe has converted many. A lovely yellow cream surrounds each mussel nestled in its own serving dish. Are you next to have your tastes changed?

Yield: 24 to 36 mussels

4 tablespoons (½ stick) unsalted butter

2 shallots, chopped

4 cloves garlic, minced

2 tablespoons finely chopped fresh parsley

1½ cups dry white wine

½ cup heavy cream

1 teaspoon curry powder

3 pounds mussels, scrubbed and debearded

Parsley, as garnish

Melt butter in a stockpot over medium-high heat. Add shallots, garlic, parsley, wine, cream, and curry powder and boil until liquid thickens, about 10 minutes. Add mussels; cover and cook until mussels open, about 5 minutes.

Remove mussels from the pot, reserving cooking liquid. Remove meats and separate the shells, saving the best for the final presentation. Place 1 mussel in each reserved shell.

Pour cooking liquid into a medium saucepan and boil over medium-high heat for a few minutes until liquid is thickened and reduced. Spoon sauce over each mussel and garnish with a parsley leaf. Serve warm or at room temperature. Ingredients may be prepared a day or two in advance; assemble and reheat just before serving.

Modify

Add 2 cups chopped fennel to sauce and omit cream. Serve by the bowlful, garnished with a large fennel frond for a light meal starter.

Magnify

Mussels are a great crowd-pleaser. People will assume you have slaved over the stove when you and I know the hardest part is debearding them. Serve a large quantity in a big bowl, add an ample supply of crusty bread to sop up the juice, and you have a ready-made party.

Sea Bass with Minted Pea Purée

Sea bass is a trendy food these days, going for top dollar in most restaurants. Admittedly, it isn't the cheapest fish at the market, but a pound goes a long way and will definitely impress your guests. Its firmness and sweetness will make this dish a hit, especially when served with these purée-topped chips.

Yield: 24 canapés

2 tablespoons extra-virgin olive oil

1 small clove garlic, minced

1 shallot, finely chopped

1 cup cooked peas

¼ cup chicken broth

2 tablespoons chopped fresh mint

Salt and freshly ground pepper

1 pound sea bass, in thick fillets or steaks

24 thick, semi-flat, good-quality unsalted potato chips

½ cup cooked peas, as garnish

Mint leaves, as garnish

Heat 1 tablespoon of the oil in a small skillet, over low heat. Add garlic and shallot. Cook until soft but not browned, about 8 minutes. Add 1 cup peas. Raise heat to medium and cook, stirring, for 3 minutes.

Transfer half the pea mixture to a food processor, add chicken broth, and pulse until smooth. Add remaining pea mixture and pulse until coarsely chopped. Add chopped mint and season with salt and pepper to taste. (Purée can be made a day ahead and kept in the refrigerator. Bring to room temperature before using.)

Heat remaining 1 tablespoon oil in a small skillet over medium-high heat. Salt and pepper sea bass and sear until golden brown, about 4 to 5 minutes on each side. Cool to room temperature.

Use a sharp knife to cut sea bass into 1-inch squares. Cooked sea bass flakes easily, so each square should yield three pieces. Spread pea purée on top of each chip, reserving a bit for garnish. Top with a piece of sea bass, then a dab of pea purée, and garnish with a few whole peas and a mint leaf or two. Serve immediately.

Modify

If sea bass is too pricey for your budget, use halibut. It is a firm fish with a very nice flavor; the pieces will just not be as thick. Place them on top of a carrot purée flavored with thyme and serve on top of blue corn tortilla chips.

Magnify

Increase sea bass to 2 pounds. Reduce peas to ½ cup and add ½ cup each chopped mango, chopped dried banana chips, and chopped fresh strawberries, and replace mint with chives. Sauté as above until banana chips have softened slightly but other fruit remains firm. Do not process; keep the peas and fruit chunky. Makes 4 servings.

Squid Ceviche

The magic of using an acidic element like lime juice to "cook" seafood has always fascinated me. Ceviche is so simple, so versatile, and so easy; the only challenge is finding very, very fresh fish (sushi grade, if possible) to do it justice. This ceviche is a classy way to entertain easily.

Yield: 20 servings

8 ounces squid, cleaned

4 ounces halibut (about 1 steak), chopped into ½- to ¾-inch pieces

4 ounces bay scallops

¼ cup very thin rings red onion, quartered

1 large clove garlic, minced

½ cup seeded chopped tomato

1 tablespoon finely chopped fresh cilantro

¼ cup fresh lime juice

1 teaspoon grated lime zest

⅛ teaspoon salt

1 mango, peeled and cut into ½- to ¾-inch pieces

¾ cup blackberries, quartered

Cilantro leaves, as garnish

Cordial or shot glasses

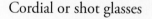

Poach squid in boiling salted water for 1 minute. Drain and cool. Slice bodies into thin rings and chop tentacles into small pieces.

Combine remaining ingredients except fruit and garnish in a medium bowl. Refrigerate, covered, for at least an hour or up to overnight. Just before serving, add mango and blackberries. Fill each glass, mounding attractively. Garnish with a cilantro leaf and serve immediately.

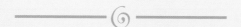

Modify

Add a finely chopped serrano chile, with or without seeds, depending on how spicy you want your ceviche to be. Squid can be omitted or replaced with shrimp or crab. With ceviche, the possibilities are endless.

Magnify

Thin slices of jicama on an appetizer plate make a crunchy foundation for strained ceviche salad. Garnish heavily with cilantro and serve as a first course with a side of freshly popped corn.

Persimmon Shrimp Bruschetta

If I had the power, I would make persimmons required eating. More popular in the South, this very sweet fruit makes a unique salsa. I favor the Fuyu persimmon because regardless of how firm or soft, it is always sweet, unlike the Hachiya persimmon, which will taste very astringent unless very, very ripe. Timing is everything!

Yield: 20 canapés

¼ cup chopped fresh cilantro

1½ tablespoons minced red onion

1 tablespoon fresh lime juice

1 teaspoon minced jalapeño pepper

3 Fuyu persimmons, peeled and coarsely chopped (about ¾ cup)

1 cup very small peeled, cooked shrimp

4 tablespoons (½ stick) unsalted butter, melted

1 tablespoon molasses

5-6 slices pumpernickel bread

Cilantro leaves, as garnish

Preheat oven to 350°F. Combine chopped cilantro, onion, lime juice, jalapeño, persimmons, and shrimp in a medium bowl and set aside.

Combine melted butter and molasses. Cut bread slices into 1½-inch squares and brush with butter mixture. Place on a baking sheet and toast in the oven for 5 to 7 minutes. Top each toast with a mound of shrimp salsa and garnish with cilantro leaves.

Modify

Replace half the cilantro with parsley and use peaches instead of persimmons. Serve on toasted whole-grain bread rounds.

Magnify

Use 1 pound medium cooked shrimp, double remaining ingredients, and serve over mesclun greens. Serves 4.

Rose Beef Canapés (page 42)

Meat Bites

For the carnivores in the crowd, the challenge in making great meat hors d'oeuvres is to make them look eminently appetizing while keeping the meat flavorful—not tough and dried out. Traditionally, meatballs and chicken wings have always been the standbys. But what if you want to create a bigger impression, offer more flavors, or just want more variety? This collection offers a tasty group of small bites in unique presentations—something to please everyone.

- Bacon Cream Rounds
- Caramelized Onion Lamb Cups
- Country Pâté Truffles
- Rose Beef Canapés
- Asian Beef Carpaccio
- Pulled Pork Scones
- Sausage Radicchio Tacos
- Bitterballen
- Venison Potato Haystacks

Bacon Cream Rounds

It was at Zambra Restaurant in Asheville, North Carolina, that I had my first memorable taste of Jerusalem artichokes. Unrelated to the standard artichoke and more like a potato, these were blended into a cream and served on thin slices of pork. The combination was unique and my taste buds have not forgotten, so in this recipe I pay homage to Chef Josh Dillard's dish by pairing bacon and Jerusalem artichoke cream purée atop a flaky, savory biscuit.

Yield: 20 rounds

10 strips bacon

8 ounces Jerusalem artichokes, peeled and chopped (about 2 cups)

Salt

½ cup heavy cream

20 Bacon Biscuits (page 122)

Parsley sprigs, as garnish

Photo: page 87

Cook bacon in a skillet over medium-high heat until crisp. Drain, crumble, and set aside. In a small saucepan, boil Jerusalem artichokes in salted water until they are tender, about 30 minutes. While artichokes are cooking, whip cream in a small bowl to stiff peaks. Drain Jerusalem artichokes and mash until smooth. Fold whipped cream into artichoke purée.

Spread a generous amount of artichoke cream on each Bacon Biscuit and crumble bacon on top. Garnish with a parsley sprig and serve warm.

Modify

If you can't find Jerusalem artichokes, mashed parsnips and/or turnips make an acceptable substitute, But don't pass up the opportunity to try the real deal: most grocers will order Jerusalem artichokes for you if asked.

Magnify

Instead of mashed potatoes, try mashed Jerusalem artichokes. Add butter and cream and fold in bacon bits before serving.

Caramelized Onion Lamb Cups

Raw onions are like Cinderella before the ball. Cook them slowly, letting their natural sugars release, until they turn sweet and golden brown. Add fresh herbs, toasted walnuts, and small pieces of lamb. Put into these lovely cups and you have food fit for a queen. Just remember to stop eating at twelve!

Yield: 16 cups

16 wonton wrappers

2 large red onions

2 tablespoons unsalted butter

1 tablespoon extra-virgin olive oil

1 bay leaf

¼ teaspoon chopped fresh rosemary

4 sprigs fresh thyme or 1 teaspoon dried

½ teaspoon salt

1 small clove garlic, finely chopped

¼ cup dry white wine

1 tablespoon walnut oil

Salt and freshly ground pepper

¼ pound lamb, cut into 1 × 3 × ½-inch strips

½ cup walnuts, toasted (page 131)

Rosemary or thyme sprigs, as garnish

Miniature muffin pan

Photo: pages 4 and 35

Preheat oven to 350°F. Gently press each wonton wrapper into a cup of an ungreased miniature muffin pan so edges are fluted and ruffled. Bake until wrappers are lightly browned but edges are not overcooked, about 8 minutes.

Slice onions as thinly and uniformly as possible so they cook evenly. Warm butter and olive oil in a medium skillet over low heat with herbs to bring out their flavor, about 1 minute. When oil is hot and herbs are fragrant, add onions. Cook slowly over low heat, stirring occasionally, until onions are golden brown and caramelized, about 20 minutes.

Add garlic and wine. Raise heat to medium and cook until wine is reduced to a syrupy consistency. Add ½ cup water and walnut oil. Stirring constantly, cook slowly until liquid is reduced by about one-third, forming a little sauce. Season with salt and pepper to taste. Discard bay leaf and any thyme sprigs.

Add lamb and cook over medium heat for a few minutes, just until the center is still a bit pink. Stir in walnuts.

Spoon about a tablespoon of filling into each wonton cup. Garnish with rosemary or thyme sprigs. Serve warm or at room temperature.

Modify

For vegetarian cups, replace lamb with chopped cooked bell pepper, carrot, zucchini, yellow squash, pea pods, peas, spinach, or eggplant—whatever is in season.

Magnify

For a vegetarian starter, simply leave out lamb and wonton wrappers, double remaining ingredients, and serve over pasta. Serves 6.

Country Pâté Truffles

A favorite hors d'oeuvre of The Penguin Rep Theatre, my local professional theater, these surprising savories are frequently served at fund-raisers or pre-show/opening parties. Covered with nuts or parsley, they look like candy until you bite inside, when they deliver the complex country pâté flavor patrons love. An addiction to these truffles won't increase your dental bills.

Yield: 30 truffles

½ onion, roughly chopped

1 clove garlic

½ pound cremini mushrooms, trimmed and halved

½ teaspoon salt

½ teaspoon freshly ground pepper

2 tablespoons chopped fresh parsley

½ teaspoon grated nutmeg

Small pinch ground cloves

Small pinch cinnamon

½ pound ground turkey

¼ pound chicken livers, trimmed

½ pound cooked ham, chopped

½ cup bread, torn into small pieces

1 tablespoon brandy

½ cup Dijon mustard

¼ cup heavy cream

2 cups finely chopped walnuts

Petit four paper baking cups or paper liners for mini muffin pans

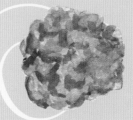

Preheat oven to 350°F. In a food processor, pulse onion and garlic until finely chopped. Add mushrooms, salt, pepper, 1 tablespoon of the parsley, and spices. Pulse until finely chopped and remove. Then place meats in processor and blend into a smooth paste. Add to mushrooms along with bread and brandy and combine well. Shape into 1-inch balls. Place on a baking sheet and bake until browned and cooked through, about 15 minutes. Set aside for 5 minutes.

Combine mustard and cream in one small bowl and the remaining 1 tablespoon parsley and walnuts in another. Using tongs, drop 5 or 6 meatballs into mustard cream and toss to coat lightly, then roll in walnuts until covered. Drop a ball into each paper cup and serve. May be served cool or at room temperature but not ice cold (or they will taste like leftovers!).

Modify

Replace ham and turkey with any leftover meals.

Magnify

Press pâté into a loaf pan and bake until cooked through, about 40 minutes, Allow to cool, then cut into thin slices and serve with Dijon mustard, cornichons, and Thyme Diamond Wafers (page 128).

Rose Beef Canapés

I've never been a sandwich eater; in fact, when my mom packed a lunch for me as a kid, I asked her to please give me just the meat! She kindly rolled it on toothpicks and sent me to school with a Baggie full. It was the balance of flavors that bothered me: too much bread and not enough meat—not to mention flavor. And that distaste for sandwiches lasted until I had a mouthful in New York City that sent my tongue into a frenzy. This sandwich had rare roast beef, red onion, arugula, and an herbed cheese spread. And that's what you'll find in these beautiful but very easy canapés.

Yield: 24 canapés

8-12 large slices whole-grain bread

4 tablespoons (½ stick) unsalted butter, melted

6 ounces whipped cream cheese

¼ cup milk

1 small clove garlic, minced

¼ cup chopped mixed fresh herbs (chives, marjoram, tarragon, and/or basil)

Salt and freshly ground pepper

1 large bunch arugula

12 thin slices rare roast beef

2 tablespoons finely chopped red onion

2-inch round cutter

Photo: pages 34 and 130

Preheat oven to 350°F. Cut two or three 2-inch rounds from each slice of bread for a total of 24 rounds.* Brush both sides of each slice with melted butter. Place on a baking sheet and toast until brown, about 12 to 15 minutes. Toasted rounds can be prepared up to 5 days in advance as long as they are kept in a sealed plastic bag in a cool place.

Blend cream cheese with milk, garlic, and herbs in a small bowl until smooth. Season with salt and pepper to taste. Spread an even layer of herbed cheese on top of each toast.

Stack several arugula leaves and roll tightly. Thinly slice the roll to create fine ribbons of arugula. Repeat with remaining arugula; you should have about 3 cups. Top each toast with a small mound of arugula.

Continued on next page

*To make use of bread scraps, see "What to Do with Leftover Bread?" in *Tastefully Small Finger Sandwiches*.

Modify

For a change of pace, use thinly sliced baked ham (remembering that it is the crusty edge that defines the rose's shape) on a mustard-based spread with a bed of raw spinach.

Magnify

To convert this recipe into a full-size appetizer course, coat baguette halves with herbed cheese, and layer with roast beef, red onion, arugula or other leafy lettuce, and capers to make a delicious sandwich.

Place 1 slice of beef on a cutting board and cut a strip down each side, 1 inch from the browned edge. Put aside the center part for another use. Take one strip and roll it up, tightly at first, then less and less so. Pinch the inside, non-dark edge of the roll. Fold down the outside edges to create petals. Finally, cut a thin slice off the bottom where you have been holding it together to create a flat base.

Nestle the rose atop the arugula and into the spread. Sprinkle a few pieces of red onion in the center of the rose. Repeat with remaining ingredients.

Canapés can be assembled in advance and refrigerated in a covered container for up to 12 hours.

Asian Beef Carpaccio (page 46)

Asian Beef Carpaccio

Raw food is trendy these days, but we forget that steak carpaccio has been around forever. This is an updated, fusion version of that classic dish, featuring finely shaved slices of steak with Asian flavors. The sesame baskets add graceful aesthetics and a sweet crunch to the experience.

Yield: 20 canapés

¼ pound very fresh, good-quality raw
sirloin steak

2 tablespoons minced chives

1 tablespoon sesame oil

20 Sesame Crisps (page 120),
formed into cups

Minced chives, as garnish

Black* and white sesame seeds, as garnish

Photo: pages 45 and 136

Place steak in freezer for half an hour. Then, using a serrated knife, shave it thinly. Stir 2 tablespoons chives into sesame oil and toss to coat slices on both sides.

Gently place a slice or two of shaved steak into each sesame cup. Garnish with minced chives and sesame seeds.

*Available in the Asian foods section of some grocery stores or at Asian specialty markets.

───────────── 6 ─────────────

Modify

Instead of sesame oil, toss steak slices with thinly shaved Parmesan. Add cracked pepper and salt to taste.

Magnify

Cook a steak medium rare and slice it thinly. Place slices on a small plate. Using a pastry bag fitted with a large star tip, pipe out mounds of cooked mashed carrots and of mashed parsnips. Sprinkle with chopped scallions and garnish with a sesame crisp.

Pulled Pork Scones

A merging of southern food traditions in one bite. A southern party staple is the classic ham biscuit; this recipe borrows liberally from that favorite and gives it more texture and flavor. Changing the biscuit to a cornmeal scone and the ham slices to a sweet, tangy pulled pork topping makes this little open-faced sandwich sure to please.

Yield: 40 scones

½ cup ketchup

1 tablespoon cider vinegar

1 tablespoon Dijon mustard

3 tablespoons molasses

2 teaspoons chipotle adobo sauce*

⅛ teaspoon freshly ground pepper

1 tablespoon vegetable oil

1 small clove garlic, forced through a garlic press

1 small onion, finely chopped

1 picnic pork shoulder with the bone (about 3 pounds)

20 Cornmeal Scones (page 124)

¾ cup crème fraîche or sour cream

2 scallions, chopped or cut into curls, as garnish

Combine ketchup, vinegar, mustard, molasses, chipotle adobo sauce, and pepper in a small bowl and set aside. Heat oil in a small saucepan over medium-high heat and cook garlic for 30 seconds, then add onion and cook for 1 minute longer. Add ketchup sauce and bring to a boil. Immediately reduce heat to medium-low and simmer for 20 minutes. Cool to room temperature. (This barbecue sauce can be kept in the refrigerator for a week. Makes 1 cup.)

Place pork in a heavy stockpot. Measure out ¼ cup of the barbecue sauce and spread on pork. Add 2 tablespoons water and cook, covered, over medium-low heat for 1½ to 2 hours or until meat can easily be pulled from the bone. Set aside until cool enough to handle, then cut into thin slices. With your fingers, pull meat into shreds. Return meat to the pot and add all the remaining sauce except for 2 tablespoons. Heat meat and sauce until warm. In a small bowl, combine reserved 2 tablespoons sauce with crème fraîche.

To assemble, split each scone in half horizontally with a fork, creating 2 scone bases. Top each scone half with a mound of warmed pulled pork. Garnish with a dollop of barbecue cream and scallions. Serve warm.

*Available in the Latin-American foods section of supermarkets and in specialty stores.

Modify

This sauce works wonderfully with other meats as well. Consider using it with pot roast or shredded chicken.

Magnify

Double sauce and pork to make an excellent pork sandwich to serve as an open-faced appetizer or with soup for an easy lunch.

Sausage Radicchio Tacos

When we were teens, my best friend Patty, and I loved tacos. At that time, the only way to get a taco was to drive half an hour to the only Jack in the Box in Bergen County, New Jersey, for deep-fried tacos. We would gorge ourselves. I can't say that we've outgrown our guilty pleasure, but our tastes have broadened. Patty and I can easily gobble up these petite and flavorful cheese tacos. Try serving this "fast food." I guarantee it will quickly disappear.

Yield: 20 mini tacos

2 cups grated Parmesan cheese (about 8 ounces)

4 cloves garlic, finely chopped

½ pound sweet Italian sausage (about 2 links)

2 cups thinly sliced radicchio (about 1 large head)

1 cup thinly sliced arugula

Salt and freshly ground pepper

Preheat oven to 350°F. Line baking sheets with silicone sheets or parchment paper. Sprinkle 1 tablespoon cheese into a 3-inch circle. Make additional circles 1 inch apart. Bake until cheese is melted and lightly browned around edges, about 8 minutes. Cool just long enough for the cheese to firm slightly and so it is not too hot to handle, about 1 minute. While they are still warm and pliable, use a small metal spatula to partially fold each round into a taco shell shape and hold until they cool and harden. Continue until you have made 20 shells. If cheese firms too much to form, return it to the oven for 30 seconds. (These can be made days in advance and kept at room temperature in an airtight container.)

Cook garlic and sausage in a skillet over medium-high heat, crumbling sausage into small pieces as it browns, about 8 minutes. Reduce heat to low and add radicchio, arugula, and salt and pepper to taste. Cook until radicchio and arugula wilt and are coated with sausage juices, about another 5 minutes. Spoon sausage filling into each taco and serve immediately.

Modify

Take the classic taco route: Use spiced ground beef, chopped onions, grated cheese, and salsa for the filling.

Magnify

Follow directions above for the filling. Sprinkle ¼ cup cheese into a 5-inch nonstick skillet over medium-low heat to soften. Spoon a fourth of the cooked filling over the melted cheese. Sprinkle another ¼ cup cheese over the filling and cook for 5 to 6 minutes or until the bottom cheese layer is golden brown. Using a wide spatula, slide this "open taco" onto a small plate and flip it back into the skillet to cook the other side until it is equally golden brown. Repeat the process with the remaining ingredients to make 4 servings. Serve warm, whole or in halves.

Bitterballen

One of the many things I loved about my dad the scientist was his willingness to try unusual recipes. For example, one Thanksgiving he replaced our traditional stuffing with oyster stuffing because he had never tried it. Another time, inspired by wild-food guru Euell Gibbons, he stuffed day lily blossoms instead. This recipe was another exploration by my dad, this time into our Dutch culinary roots. These delicate-tasting meatballs, still a popular snack in Holland, were one of the best dishes my dad ever made. I hope my own experimental track record turns out at least as good.

Yield: 35 meatballs

3 tablespoons unsalted butter

5 tablespoons flour

1 cup chicken broth

½ pound ground veal

1 tablespoon finely chopped fresh parsley

1 tablespoon Dijon mustard

½ teaspoon salt

Freshly ground pepper

1 teaspoon Worcestershire sauce

Vegetable oil for frying

2 egg whites

1 cup fine dry bread crumbs

4 or 5 long carrots, peeled

Decorative toothpicks

Heat butter in a small saucepan over medium heat. Add flour and stir into a paste, cooking for 2 minutes. Gradually add broth and cook for a few minutes longer, stirring constantly, until a thick paste has formed. Place in a bowl and cool slightly. Add veal, parsley, mustard, salt, pepper, and Worcestershire sauce and mix thoroughly. Refrigerate until firm, about 2 hours.

Whisk egg whites in a shallow bowl just until frothy. Place bread crumbs in another shallow bowl. Roll meat into 1-inch balls. Dip balls in egg whites, then roll in bread crumbs. Heat ½ to ¾ inch oil in a medium skillet over medium-high heat until almost smoking. Add meatballs, in batches if necessary, and fry until they are golden brown, about 2 minutes. Drain on paper towels.

Using a vegetable peeler, cut long thin slices of carrot from the whole carrots. Blanch carrot strips to soften slightly (see page 132). To garnish, wrap each warm meatball with a carrot strip and secure with a toothpick.

Modify

Cook the meatballs plain, without the egg white dip and bread crumbs. Roll lightly in mustard diluted with water to make the surface sticky, then roll in chopped parsley or finely grated carrots.

Magnify

Double recipe and shape meat into 3- to 4-inch ovals. Deep-fry and serve 2 per appetizer plate with a sprinkle of parsley and a small dish of mustard.

Venison Potato Haystacks

Growing up in the New York area, I was very familiar with potato latkes and kugel. Unfortunately, both usually lacked the crispness and the flavor I was promised. Then it dawned on me: fried latkes were really only small amounts of potato kugel, which was traditionally baked. Could I get the crispness of those little latkes without having to go through the trouble of frying them? The answer is yes! Now I have the crispness without the greasy mess, plus lots of flavor when meat is added.

Yield: 25 haystacks

2 to 3 medium potatoes, peeled

¼ cup finely chopped onion (about ½ medium onion)

6 ounces cooked venison, shredded or chopped

1 large egg

1 tablespoon flour

4 tablespoons (½ stick) unsalted butter, melted

½ teaspoon salt

¼ teaspoon freshly ground pepper

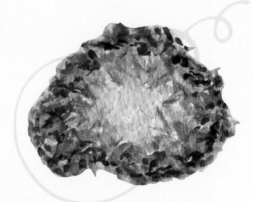

Preheat oven to 400°F. Line 2 baking sheets with silicone sheets or parchment paper. Grate potatoes on the largest holes of a box grater or with a food processor to yield 2 packed cups. Place potatoes in a cotton dish towel and squeeze as much liquid from them as possible. Set aside for 5 to 10 minutes.

Combine onion, venison, egg, flour, butter, salt, and pepper in a medium bowl. Stir in potatoes. Spoon heaping tablespoonfuls onto each baking sheet, 1½ inches apart. Bake until both tops and bottoms are crisp and brown, about 20 minutes. Serve immediately. Haystacks can be made a day in advance, kept refrigerated, and recrisped for a few minutes at 400°F.

Modify

Replace venison with crumbled pork sausage and 1 teaspoon finely chopped rosemary or with colorful grated vegetables, e.g., yellow squash, carrot, and/or zucchini.

Magnify

Spoon out twice as much potato to make mounds twice as large. Press each mound down with a spatula to flatten and bake for an extra 5 minutes until brown and crispy. Serve 2 or 3 per person, topped with sour cream and caviar for an elegant appetizer.

Pecan Sweet Potato Thumbprints

My uncle would always say, "I never met a potato I didn't like." I could say that about sweet potatoes. Don't leave your sweet potatoes on the counter if I'm around unless you're trying to feed me. These two-bite morsels are a simple sweet potato salad with ham cradled in a nest of crispy pecans. What's not to like?

Yield: 24 bites

Dough for 24 Pecan Mounds (page 123)

2½ cups peeled sweet potatoes in small dice

2 tablespoons mayonnaise

1 scallion, white and green parts, chopped

1 cup diced cooked ham

¼ teaspoon salt

Freshly ground pepper

Pecans, chopped, as garnish

Prepare Pecan Mounds as directed, pressing a well into each mound with your thumb before baking.

Boil sweet potatoes in salted water in a medium saucepan, until tender but still holding their shape, about 12 minutes. Drain. Cool completely in a small bowl.

Gently stir in remaining ingredients except pecans. Scoop by the teaspoon into the Pecan Mounds and sprinkle with pecans to garnish.

This salad can be made a day in advance and kept in an air tight container in the refrigerator.

Modify

Cook sweet potatoes with ham and 1 cup chopped tart apple in a covered casserole dish at 350°F until sweet potatoes and apples are soft. Scoop into Pecan Mounds for a variation with an edge.

Magnify

Cut 1 pound cooked ham and 3 medium sweet potatoes into French fry–size strips. Boil sweet potatoes until soft and mix with ham, 2 scallions julienned to matchstick size, and ½ cup halved pecans. Divide equally among 4 butter lettuce cups. Drizzle on ¼ cup mayonnaise thinned with milk. Sprinkle on chopped rosemary for a finishing touch.

Chicken Artichoke Bites (page 70)

Poultry and Egg Bites

Poultry, especially chicken, is the most popular meat. Aren't people always saying, "It tastes like chicken"? Other birds, like duck and turkey are just as tasty, are readily available in most markets, and add a touch of elegance to creative hors d'oeuvres. See if your discriminating guests don't agree.

- Pomegranate Chicken Purses
- Turkey Cranberry Relish Scoops
- Waffled Ginger Duck
- Lemon Caper Chicken Cups
- Chicken Artichoke Bites
- Polka Dot Squares
- Deviled Guacamole Cups

Pomegranate Chicken Purses

My friend Kat, for a cookbook editing class, had to write her own recipe. And I copied her homework—miniaturized, of course. The "gold" in this purse is pomegranate-flavored chicken, a sweet-sour combination that works perfectly as a starter bite.

Yield: 12 purses

1 tablespoon extra-virgin olive oil

2 tablespoons unsalted butter

1 skinless, boneless chicken breast, chopped into 1-inch pieces

1 skinless, boneless chicken thigh, chopped into 1-inch pieces

2 tablespoons minced onion

1 clove garlic, minced

¼ cup unsweetened pomegranate juice

¼ cup honey

¼ cup pomegranate seeds

4 or 5 sheets phyllo dough

8 tablespoons (1 stick) unsalted butter, melted

Melt olive oil with 1 tablespoon of the butter in a skillet over medium heat. Add chicken and cook for 6 to 7 minutes or until browned and no longer pink inside. Remove from skillet and set aside; add remaining 1 tablespoon butter, onion, and garlic to the skillet. Cook until onion is caramelized. Add pomegranate juice and honey and continue to cook until liquid is reduced by half, about 10 minutes. Chop chicken into small dice, stir into sauce, and set aside.

Line 2 baking sheets with parchment paper. Preheat oven to 400°F. Unroll phyllo dough onto a flat surface. Cover phyllo with a layer of plastic wrap and a dampened towel to prevent the sheets from drying out. Place 1 sheet on a flat surface and brush entire surface lightly with melted butter. Cut sheet into 9 equal squares, discarding any leftover phyllo (usually about a 2-inch strip). Stack 3 squares on top of each other in an irregular fashion, then mound a tablespoon of chicken filling in the center. Sprinkle a few pomegranate seeds on top. With your fingertips, gently lift phyllo dough corners and pinch "purse" shut, leaving phyllo edges ruffled. Place purse onto baking sheet and repeat until filling has been used up. Bake until phyllo is browned, making sure ruffles don't burn, about 5 to 7 minutes.

Modify

Omit the pomegranate juice and seeds. Increase honey to ⅓ cup and mix in 2 teaspoons curry powder.

Magnify

Layer the bottom of a medium glass baking dish with slices of 1 medium onion and place 4 chicken breasts on top. Salt and pepper the chicken. Whisk together ½ cup honey, ½ cup pomegranate juice, and 2 minced cloves garlic and brush on the chicken. Bake at 375°F, recoating the chicken pieces after 10 minutes with the remaining glaze, until chicken is cooked through, about 20 to 30 minutes. Serves 4.

Turkey Cranberry Relish Scoops

This refreshing relish came about when my sister made a wonderful gelatin salad for dessert on Thanksgiving. Cranberry is a favorite flavor for both of us, but this dessert was more refreshing and flavorful than any cranberry combination I'd had before. A few changes later, these traditional ingredients have a new life in these festive bites for any holiday party.

Yield: 24 scoops

1½ cups diced cooked turkey

1 teaspoon chopped fresh thyme or ½ teaspoon dried

½ cup pineapple chunks, fresh or canned, drained

1 teaspoon fresh lemon juice

1 stalk celery, cut into chunks

½ apple, unpeeled, cored, and cut into ½-inch chunks

1 cup fresh or frozen cranberries

½ orange, peeled, seeded, and coarsely chopped

2 tablespoons honey

24 endive leaves

Thyme sprigs, as garnish

Photo: pages 3 and 69

Toss turkey and thyme in a small bowl. Pulse remaining ingredients except endive in a food processor until puréed. (Relish can be made a few days in advance and kept covered in the refrigerator.) Spoon onto the base of each endive leaf, top with diced turkey, and garnish with a little more relish and a thyme sprig.

Modify

Even frozen cranberries can be hard to find, so stock up when in season. Plumped dried cranberries will also work, or raspberries. For variety, replace endive with mini bok choy, or cranberries with 1½ cups blackberries or strawberries.

Magnify

Leftover turkey or roasted chicken makes a wonderful lunch dish when topped with warmed cranberry relish. The contrast of sweet meat and tart sauce is delicious. Serves 3.

Waffled Ginger Duck

Duck breast is an elegant, tasty meat that everyone loves and thinks is difficult to prepare. Relax. Paired with a crunchy waffle and ginger-maple syrup, duck is dramatic yet simple. My Dutch ancestors would be proud of the traditional waffle used in such an innovative way.

Yield: 16 to 20 waffle bites

1 cup flour

1 tablespoon sugar

½ teaspoon baking powder

½ teaspoon baking soda

½ teaspoon salt

1 teaspoon ground ginger

1 tablespoon ground cinnamon

½ teaspoon ground cardamom

⅛ teaspoon ground cloves

2 eggs

3 tablespoons unsalted butter, melted and cooled

½ cup whole milk

½ cup sour cream

2 tablespoons molasses

2 duck breasts

Salt and freshly ground pepper

1 teaspoon juniper berries

½ teaspoon minced garlic

1 teaspoon finely chopped green scallions

2 tablespoons ginger syrup

¼ cup maple syrup

Chopped chives, as garnish

Waffle iron

Whisk dry ingredients together in a medium bowl. In a separate bowl, whisk together eggs, butter, milk, sour cream, and molasses. Add to dry ingredients and whisk until smooth.

Heat waffle iron, add ⅓ cup batter, and cook until golden brown. Repeat with remaining batter. Cut each waffle into quarters.

Pat duck breasts dry and salt and pepper both sides. Sauté duck in a skillet over medium-high heat, skin side down, for 10 minutes, until skin is crisp and golden and most of the fat has rendered out. Turn duck breasts over and continue to cook until duck is cooked through but slightly pink in the center, about 5 minutes. Cool to room temperature. Remove skin if desired and cut into thin slices.

Grind juniper berries with a mortar and pestle or in a clean coffee grinder. Combine in a small bowl with remaining ingredients except chives.

Place 2 to 3 small slices of duck on top of each waffle square. Drizzle with ginger-maple syrup. Sprinkle with chives and serve warm or at room temperature.

Modify

Use barbecue sauce on page 48 instead of ginger-maple syrup. Slather on duck and roast at 400°F for about 8 minutes. Slice thinly, place on pumpernickel toast (see page 33), and top with chives.

Magnify

Omit waffles, double remaining recipe, and divide duck slices among 4 plates over a bed of torn radicchio and endive. Sprinkle with crumbled pieces of gingerbread cookies and toasted hazelnut halves and drizzle with syrup.

Lemon Caper Chicken Cups

Two dishes from two different parts of the world have always been favorites of mine: Chinese lemon chicken and chicken piccata. Both are usually prepared too mildly for my taste—except at a restaurant in New York's Chinatown. This little "hole in the wall" would use pieces of lemon, skin and all, including the pith! The place is long gone, but the memory lingers. Using the whole lemon in piccata was just the punch I was looking for. And this small crêpe cup is packed with it.

Yield: 24 cups

2 cups flour

2 eggs

2 egg whites

2 cups milk

1 teaspoon sugar

1 teaspoon salt

Unsalted butter, melted, for crêpe pan

1 large lemon

1 pound chicken tenders

¼ teaspoon salt

⅛ teaspoon freshly ground pepper

¼ cup flour

2 tablespoons vegetable oil

1 small clove garlic, minced

½ cup chicken stock

1 tablespoon small capers

1 tablespoon unsalted butter, softened

2 tablespoons chopped fresh parsley, optional

Parsley leaves, as garnish

3-inch round cutter

Miniature muffin pan

To make the crêpes: Combine 2 cups flour, eggs, and whites in a medium bowl and whisk until smooth. Add milk, sugar, and salt and combine. Set batter aside to rest for 30 minutes to 1 hour.

Heat a crêpe pan or small nonstick skillet over medium-high heat and brush with a little melted butter to coat. Pour in ¼ cup batter. Swirl pan until a very thin, even layer of batter coats the entire bottom of the pan. Cook for about 5 minutes or until the underside is lightly browned. Turn crêpe over and cook for another minute. Slide crêpe onto a plate and continue the process with remaining batter.

Preheat oven to 350°F. Cut out 2 or 3 rounds from each crêpe. Press rounds firmly into muffin pan cups. Bake until lightly browned and stiff, about 8 minutes. Cool. (Shells can be prepared a few days in advance and kept in a cool, airtight container or frozen.) If you wish, cut out decorative shapes from crêpe scraps using aspic or tiny cookie cutters, bake for 1 to 2 minutes, and set aside for garnish.

Peel and mince zest from half the lemon. Squeeze juice into a small bowl and set aside. Remove seeds from and finely chop the remaining half lemon, including skin and pith.

Continued on next page

Modify

Replace capers, lemon juice, and zest with ½ cup chopped mushrooms.

Magnify

Increase chicken to 4 boneless, skinless breasts (about 1½ pounds), pounded into cutlets. Coat lightly with flour, salt and pepper, and sauté until lightly browned on both sides. Omit crêpes but double sauce for a delicious main meal or tasty first course for 4.

Cut chicken tenders into ½-inch pieces. Pour salt, pepper, and ¼ cup flour into a plastic bag. Add chicken pieces and shake to coat.

Heat oil in a skillet over medium-high heat. Add chicken in 1 layer and cook for 2 minutes without stirring. Turn chicken over and cook for another minute until browned and no longer pink inside, about 2 minutes longer. Remove from skillet and set aside. Add garlic to skillet and cook for 30 seconds. Add stock and 2 tablespoons chopped lemon. Increase heat to high and scrape skillet until brown bits are released. Boil until liquid is reduced by half, about 2 minutes. Add lemon juice, zest, and capers and boil until sauce is again reduced by half, about 1 minute longer. Return chicken to pan and cook for 1 minute longer, just until chicken is heated through and coated with sauce. Remove skillet from heat and swirl in butter to thicken sauce. Add chopped parsley if desired.

Fill each crêpe cup with chicken and garnish with a crêpe shape or parsley leaf.

Turkey Cranberry Relish Scoops (page 62)

Chicken Artichoke Bites

Until I was in my twenties, the only artichoke I'd ever seen was on The Little Rascals: *Alfalfa keeps pushing down the leaves, looking for the edible part. Fortunately, one day my boss took me out for artichokes. I've been in love with the delicate flavor ever since.*

Yield: 36 bites

2 large fresh artichokes

8 ounces frozen artichoke hearts

2 cups chicken broth

1 clove garlic, minced

2 shallots, minced

1 tablespoon vegetable oil

4 tablespoons (½ stick) unsalted butter

Salt and freshly ground pepper

2 skinless, boneless chicken breasts, cut into 1-inch pieces

½ cup dry white wine

5 teaspoons minced fresh basil or 1½ teaspoons dried

½ cup shelled, finely chopped unsalted pistachio nuts, as garnish

½ cup thinly sliced fresh basil, as garnish

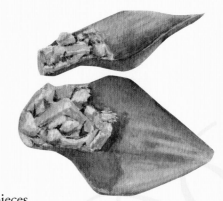

Photo: page 58

Trim ¼ inch off artichoke stems. Remove the outermost leaves and, using scissors, snip tips of remaining outer leaves. Spread out leaves slightly and place facedown in a steaming basket in a large saucepan over boiling water. Cover and steam over medium-high heat until tender, about 30 to 40 minutes. Cool. Pull off 36 leaves. Remove chokes, trim and chop hearts, and set aside.

Simmer frozen artichoke hearts in broth in a small saucepan for 15 minutes. Drain and discard broth or save for another use.

Sauté garlic and shallots in oil and 1 tablespoon of the butter, in a large skillet over medium-high heat, stirring for 1 minute. Salt and pepper chicken breasts. Add to the pan and cook, stirring, until chicken is no longer pink in the center, about 5 minutes. Add wine and minced basil and bring to a boil. Remove from heat and stir in remaining 3 tablespoons butter. Season with salt and pepper to taste and cool.

Pulse simmered and steamed artichoke hearts in a food processor until coarsely chopped. Remove to a bowl. Pulse chicken and its cooking liquid until finely chopped but not puréed. Add chicken to artichokes and stir well to combine.

To assemble, place a tablespoon of chicken filling onto the tender part of each artichoke leaf. Sprinkle pistachio nuts and basil strips on top. Serve warm or at room temperature.

Modify

Replace chicken with shrimp.

Magnify

Pile filling in the center of a round plate, surrounded by artichoke leaves like a sunflower, or for a simpler alternative, cut chicken into strips instead of 1-inch pieces, cook, and serve over artichoke hearts with sauce drizzled on top. Makes 3 small plates.

Polka Dot Squares

When I eat these dice-like squares, I think "brunch in a box" because I can taste fluffy eggs, vegetable, and a bit of meat. Basically a frittata cut small and wrapped with ham, these small hors d'oeuvres will liven up any occasion. Try your luck!

Yield: 36 squares

1 pound thin asparagus, tough ends discarded

6 eggs

8 ounces cream cheese, softened

3 tablespoons flour

3 tablespoons grated Parmesan cheese

Salt and freshly ground pepper

6 slices ham, ⅛ inch thick

Preheat oven to 350°F. Line an 8-inch square cake pan with foil and spray foil with nonstick cooking spray. Place 1 layer of asparagus spears side by side loosely, alternating tips.

In a food processor or blender, blend remaining ingredients except ham until smooth. Pour just enough batter into pan to barely cover asparagus. Place another layer of the remaining asparagus, in the same fashion as above, on top, then cover with remaining batter.

Bake until firm to the touch and golden brown, about 45 minutes. Cool to room temperature.

Remove from pan and cut into 6 equal 8-inch-long strips. Wrap 1 slice ham around each strip The ends will stick out. Trim ham so that it goes around the strip exactly once with minimal overlap. Slice the wrapped part of the strip into 6 equal squares. Egg squares can be prepared and refrigerated for up to a day in advance, but bring to room temperature before serving.

Modify

Nova smoked salmon makes a tasty and pretty alternative wrapping.

Magnify

Chop asparagus and place ¼ cup at the bottom of small prebaked puff pastry shells. Pour batter over asparagus to ¼ inch from the top. Bake at 350°F until tops are golden brown. Serves 4.

Deviled Guacamole Cups

More than just deviled eggs, the bright green and yellow filling in these pure white cups is a proclamation of spring.

Yield: 20 egg cups

20 hard-boiled eggs

4 slices bacon, fried and crumbled

¼ cup whole shelled pumpkin seeds, coarsely ground

1 avocado, peeled and pitted

3 tablespoons minced scallions
(about 2 scallions white and green parts)

1 tablespoon fresh lemon juice

Salt and freshly ground pepper

⅓ cup corn kernels, fresh or frozen

Whole shelled pumpkin seeds, as garnish

Peel eggs. Cut just enough of the narrow end of each egg to remove the yolk without damaging the remaining white. Reserve three yokes and all egg white trimmings. Cut just enough off the wide end of each egg so it can stand upright. Trim cup edges decoratively if desired.

Place bacon, egg yolks and trimmings, avocado, scallions, pumpkin seeds, lemon juice, salt, and pepper in a medium bowl. Using a potato masher, roughly mash filling so that it is in small chunks. Stir in corn. Spoon filling into egg cups and garnish with whole pumpkin seeds. Cups can be assembled and refrigerated for up to a day before serving.

Modify

Use this filling in triangle finger sandwiches. For decorative edges, reserve 2 more egg yolks and mash with a little bit of milk. Using a small spatula, coat sandwich edges with a thin coat of paste and press into chopped parsley or pumpkin seeds.

Magnify

Double recipe but replace the bacon with ½ cup chopped smoked salmon. Spoon into Bibb lettuce cups to serve 8 as an appetizer you eat with your hands.

Ginger Carrot Flan (page 80); Mini Crab Cheesecakes (page 14)

Vegetable Bites

Every hors d'oeuvre assortment should include at least one vegetable bite.
Not only for dieters and vegetarians, their color, texture and diverse flavors add
welcome dimension to your spread.

- Broccoli Soufflés
- Ginger Carrot Flan
- Polenta-Stuffed Baby Bellas
- Pecan Sweet Potato Thumbprints
- Hazelnut-Crusted Brussels Sprouts
- Mac 'n' Cheese Tomatoes
- Roasted Cauliflower with Blueberry Drizzle
- Carrot Parsnip Latkes
- Mozzarella Stacks
- Zucchini Spirals
- Olé Canapés

Broccoli Soufflés

My friend Susanna is the slowest eater I know. However, I discovered while testing this recipe that if she truly loves something, she'll waste no time enjoying it. I left a pan of these mini soufflés in the kitchen only to find, minutes later, half of them gone. You should be so lucky! And there's only one way to find out.

Yield: 44 to 48 mini soufflés

3 egg yolks

½ teaspoon salt

3 tablespoons extra-virgin olive oil

2 tablespoons flour

2 tablespoon minced shallots

1½ cups half-and-half

1½ teaspoons minced fresh rosemary
or ½ teaspoon dried

1 tablespoon minced fresh thyme
or 1 teaspoon dried

1½ teaspoons minced fresh basil
or ½ teaspoon dried

1 cup blanched broccoli florets,
finely chopped (page 132)

1 cup finely grated white Cheddar cheese
(about 4 ounces)

4 egg whites

Blanched broccoli florets, as garnish

Miniature muffin pans

Foil candy cups or mini muffin pan liners
(do not use paper liners)

Photo: pages 87 and 130

78

Preheat oven to 400°F. Line muffin pans with foil cups and spray with nonstick cooking spray. Stir together egg yolks and salt in a small bowl and set aside. Heat olive oil in a medium saucepan, over medium heat. Add flour and shallots, creating a roux; cook until roux starts to bubble but not brown, stirring occasionally, 2 to 3 minutes. Gradually whisk in half-and-half and cook until thick, whisking constantly, about 2 minutes. Remove from heat. Stir ½ cup into the egg yolks, then pour that back into the saucepan, whisking to blend. Fold in herbs, broccoli, and cheese. Cool to room temperature in a large bowl.

Beat egg whites in another large bowl until they are stiff but not dry. Gently fold into broccoli-cheese mixture in two stages. Spoon evenly into muffin pans, filling each cup up to the rim. Reduce temperature to 375°F and place pan in the center of the oven. Bake until soufflés puff and are golden brown, about 15 to 18 minutes. Soufflés will deflate a bit when taken from the oven, but your garnish will hide any indentation.

Garnish with a small broccoli floret and serve immediately.

Modify

To change the flavor, use blanched, chopped cauliflower instead of broccoli. Note: The key to keeping your soufflés light and fluffy, no matter what size, is to incorporate as much air into the mix as you can. That's done by folding the egg whites in with as few strokes as possible.

Magnify

Double recipe, pour into an 8-cup soufflé dish, and bake for 35 to 40 minutes. Serve immediately.

Ginger Carrot Flan

At first glance, this little flan looks like a pretty, peach-colored dessert. But it is as savory as it is easy to make. Share the first secret; keep the second.

Yield: 18 flans

3 carrots, peeled and sliced (about 1 cup)

3 eggs

1 cup heavy cream

¼ teaspoon salt

⅛ teaspoon ground white pepper

½ teaspoon ground ginger

2 carrots, peeled and cut into small dice

1½ teaspoons grated fresh ginger

1 tablespoon brown sugar

2 tablespoons unsalted butter

Miniature muffin pan

Miniature muffin papers

Photo: page 76

Preheat oven to 325°F. Butter muffin pan. Boil sliced carrots in salted water to cover until soft. Drain.

In a food processor, pulse eggs, cream, salt, pepper, ground ginger, and cooked carrots until smooth. Press purée through a fine sieve. Spoon out 2 tablespoons per muffin pan cup. Place muffin pan onto a larger sheet pan, place onto center oven rack, and fill the sheet pan with hot water to partially immerse muffin pan. Bake until flan puffs up a bit and a toothpick inserted comes out clean, about 20 minutes.

While flans are cooking, combine remaining ingredients in a small skillet and cook over medium heat until carrots are glazed but still slightly firm.

Cool flans for a few minutes, then slide a blunt knife or small spatula carefully around the edge of each flan to release it. Remove each flan and place onto a flattened muffin paper. Spoon glazed carrots on top. Serve at room temperature.

Modify

Replacing the carrots with tender peas will alter this flan's character quite a bit. Serve alone or with an herb garnish.

Magnify

Double ingredients and ladle into 6 buttered ramekins. Bake until slightly puffed, about 30 minutes. Meanwhile, slice one carrot and one parsnip and sauté in butter, 1 tablespoon grated fresh ginger, and the zest and juice of 1 lime. Pile atop each flan.

Polenta-Stuffed Baby Bellas

On my way to the theater in New York, I stopped into a restaurant for a bite. "Glazed portabella" looked good; the polenta they brought it to me on did not. I got through half the dish saying, "Why do I love this? I usually hate polenta." The other half, I concentrated on eating. These little versions of that dish, sure to win over the polenta haters, are a tough act to follow.

Yield: about 16 mushrooms

2 tablespoons unsalted butter

1 teaspoon minced garlic

1 tablespoon balsamic vinegar

2 teaspoons brown sugar

¼ teaspoon salt

⅛ teaspoon freshly ground pepper

1½ teaspoons grated fresh ginger

2 tablespoons extra-virgin olive oil

10 ounces baby portabella (cremini) mushrooms (about sixteen, 1½ to 2 inches in diameter)

¼ cup milk

Pinch salt

¼ cup cornmeal

¼ cup grated Parmesan cheese

½ cup balsamic syrup*, as garnish

Photo: pages 77 and 87

Melt butter in a small skillet over medium heat and add garlic. Cook for 2 minutes until soft. Add vinegar, brown sugar, salt, pepper, and ginger; cook over medium heat until ginger glaze becomes syrupy and smooth, about 2 minutes. Take pan off heat, stir in olive oil, and set aside.

Preheat oven to 350°F. Line a baking sheet with parchment. Clean mushroom caps and remove stems. Brush cap inside and out with ginger glaze. Place on sheet and bake until mushrooms are tender but not mushy, about 10 minutes. Cool, then pour out any liquid that has collected in caps and dab with paper towel to dry.

Whisk milk, ½ cup water, salt, and cornmeal in a small saucepan. Cook over medium heat, stirring constantly, until polenta thickens and loses its gritty texture, about 15 to 20 minutes. Stir in Parmesan and cook until cheese has melted, about 1 minute.

Fill mushroom caps with hot polenta. Immediately drizzle balsamic syrup over polenta in a decorative manner. Serve warm or at room temperature.

*To make your own balsamic syrup, heat 2 cups (or a 17-ounce bottle) balsamic vinegar in a saucepan over high heat until it reduces to ½ cup of sticky syrup, about 25 minutes.

Modify

Add ½ teaspoon dried thyme and/or rosemary to the polenta, with or without the cheese. Very tasty.

Magnify

For large appetizers for 4, double the balsamic syrup and triple the polenta. Plate by spooning the polenta onto the plate in a large puddle, place the portabella mushrooms cap side down in the center, and garnish with a few herbs.

Hazelnut-Crusted Brussels Sprouts

I grew up hating Brussels sprouts. My dad would eat them with liver while everyone else, thankfully, got spaghetti. Now I see that these tender little cabbages, fresh off the stalk, are a far cry from their canned counterparts. If only liver were a question of freshness…

Yield: 40 sprouts

40 tender young Brussels sprouts

1½ cups panko* bread crumbs

½ cup finely chopped hazelnuts

1 egg

Flour for dredging

Vegetable oil for frying

1 large clove garlic, thinly sliced

Bring Brussels sprouts to a boil in salted water in a medium saucepan over high heat. Boil until tender, about 5 minutes. Drain well.

Mix bread crumbs and hazelnuts in a small bowl. Beat egg with a bit of water in a shallow dish. Place ½ inch flour in another shallow dish. Dip sprouts, 3 or 4 at a time, in flour to coat, then roll in egg until surface is just sticky, then finally in bread crumb/nut mix. Set aside for 10 minutes so breading adheres.

Continued on next page

*Panko are very crisp Japanese bread crumbs available in the Asian foods section of some grocery stores or at Asian specialty markets.

Modify

Chop sprouts into ¼-inch pieces. Toss with chopped pecans and grated white Cheddar cheese. Spoon a tablespoon onto the center of a 2-inch square of puff pastry. Enclose filling by pinching pastry corners together, then sealing adjacent edges. Repeat with the rest of the Brussels sprouts. Brush with egg wash (see page 133) and bake at 375 °F until golden brown.

Magnify

Steam quartered Brussels sprouts until just tender. Toss with 1 cup roughly chopped hazelnuts or cooked chestnuts and 1 cup herbed croutons. Drizzle with melted butter and serve as a side dish for 4.

Heat ½ inch oil in a small skillet over high heat until the surface is shimmering hot but not smoking, then lower heat to medium-high. Add garlic slices and cook until they have browned, about 30 seconds. Remove them at once with a slotted spoon so they do not burn. Place a few sprouts into the hot oil and brown them quickly. This will take less than a minute. Drain on paper towels and continue with remaining sprouts. Serve immediately.

These crusted sprouts can also be baked. Coat as directed, spray with a little olive oil, and bake at 375°F until browned, about 15 to 20 minutes. The crust just won't brown as deeply as when fried.

Polenta-Stuffed Baby Bellas (page 82); Bacon Cream Rounds (page 36); Broccoli Soufflés (page 78)

Mac 'n' Cheese Tomatoes

People fought over my grandmother's macaroni and cheese. Since her passing, my sister has carried on the tradition, making enough for everyone. That recipe was and is quite simple, making it no less delicious. This modern version, easier to partition, goes out in her honor.

Yield: 24 cherry tomatoes

4 ounces (1 cup) orzo

2 tablespoons unsalted butter

2 tablespoons flour

1 teaspoon dry mustard

½ teaspoon salt

Freshly ground pepper

1½ cups whole milk

2 cups grated sharp Cheddar cheese (8 ounces)

24 large cherry tomatoes

Parsley, as garnish

Cook orzo al dente and set aside. Preheat oven to 350°F.

Melt butter in a small saucepan over medium heat; whisk in flour, mustard, salt, and pepper until it forms a roux. Slowly, while whisking, pour milk into roux and cook over medium heat, stirring frequently, until sauce thickens a bit, about 3 minutes. Take pan off heat, add about two-thirds of the cheese, and whisk until cheese is incorporated. Place pan back over medium heat and bring to a boil. Pour over orzo and stir to combine. (If making filling ahead of time, cool to room temperature, then refrigerate until ready to use.)

Using a small serrated knife, slice the top third off cherry tomatoes. With a small melon baller, scoop out the insides. Fill each shell with cheese filling, mounding the tops. Place filled tomatoes in a glass baking dish, sprinkle remaining cheese over them, and bake until tomatoes and pasta are hot and the top is browned, about 20 minutes. Tops can be further browned under the broiler for a couple of minutes. Garnish with parsley and serve warm or at room temperature.

Modify

Vary cheeses for different flavors or add pieces of lobster or ham for a change of pace.

Magnify

Double orzo and cheese sauce. Halve several regular-size tomatoes, remove seeds, and slice thinly. Cut 6 large rounds from 6 firm white bread slices, spread with butter, and sprinkle liberally with Parmesan cheese. Toast in a 400°F oven until brown and crisp. Place a few tomatoe slices on each toasted round, then mound with orzo/cheese and top with extra cheese and toasted bread crumbs. Heat in oven until cheese topping melts. A great starter for 6 with soup or stew.

Roasted Cauliflower with Blueberry Drizzle

Cauliflower is one of those vegetables that gets short shrift, but this unlikely combination is both striking and delicious. And did I mention easy? The syrup has the distinctive character of blueberry without the sweetness and a touch of tartness that complements the neutrality of the cauliflower.

Yield: 24 pieces

1 large head cauliflower, broken into 1½-inch florets

2 tablespoons extra-virgin olive oil

½ teaspoon salt

¼ teaspoon freshly ground pepper

1 large clove garlic, finely chopped

1 cup frozen unsweetened blueberries, thawed, including any liquid

1 teaspoon fresh lemon juice

2 tablespoons unsalted butter

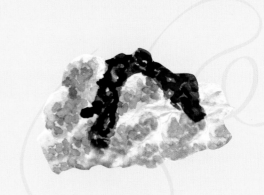

Preheat oven to 400°F. Cut each floret in half. Combine oil, salt, and pepper in a medium bowl; toss and rub the florets in the flavored oil until coated. Place florets flat side down on an ungreased baking sheet. Sprinkle chopped garlic over cauliflower and roast until florets are tender and browned, about 35 minutes.

While cauliflower is roasting, bring blueberries and their liquid to a boil in a small saucepan over high heat. Press berries into a sieve to strain out juice. Discard berries and bring juice to a boil, cooking until it is reduced by a third. Add lemon juice. Take pan off heat and whisk in butter in two stages, stirring until melted. Let sauce cool and thicken while the cauliflower finishes cooking.

To serve, place florets flat side down on a tray and drizzle blueberry sauce over the top. Serve warm or at room temperature. Sauce can be made up to 2 days in advance; cauliflower can be roasted a day in advance and reheated just before serving.

Modify

Dredge cauliflower florets in a mixture of 2 beaten eggs, 1 tablespoon water, and salt and pepper to taste. Roll each piece in grated Parmesan. Fry in small batches in ⅓ cup hot olive oil until crisp and browned. Serve hot.

Magnify

Steam a head of cauliflower until tender and serve half with blueberry sauce and half with cheese sauce (see page 88 and replace Cheddar with Parmesan).

Carrot Parsnip Latkes

Latkes are simple, classic, and comforting. Using carrot and parsnip in place of potato adds novelty, while black olives give just the right salty spike to these little pancakes.

Yield: 28 latkes

2 medium carrots, peeled

2 medium parsnips, peeled

3 eggs, lightly beaten

3 tablespoons flour

½ teaspoon salt

1 tablespoon fresh lemon juice

½ cup pitted chopped black olives

6 tablespoons extra-virgin olive oil

Mayonnaise, chopped chives, and black olive slices, as garnish

Grate carrots and parsnips on the medium holes of a box grater or with a food processor. Combine with eggs, flour, salt, lemon juice, and chopped olives in a medium bowl.

Heat oil in a heavy skillet over medium-high heat. Drop mounded tablespoons of batter into oil. Press mounds down to 2-inch pancakes. Fry about 1 minute per side until brown and crispy. Place on paper towels to drain. Keep warm until ready to serve.

Top with a small dollop of mayonnaise, a sprinkle of chives, and a slice of black olive. Serve warm.

———————— 6 ————————

Modify

Sauté ½ cup chopped porcini mushrooms and 1 small clove minced garlic. Replace carrots and parsnips with russet potatoes. After grating, squeeze as much liquid from the potatoes as possible. Add mushrooms and garlic to potatoes and omit lemon juice, olives, and garnish.

Magnify

To serve 4, double recipe. Pipe mayonnaise in ribbons across the plate before placing the latkes on top. Sprinkle olive slices and carrot curls on top as an attractive garnish. Serve warm.

Mozzarella Stacks

I never really appreciated fresh mozzarella until Chef Jason Truckenmiller of Laguna Niguel, California, served me his homemade version. Its simple rich flavor was quite removed from the firm yet bland mozzarella typically used on pizza. I'm not sure the Ritz-Carlton would ever serve this finger-food version, but here's a tribute to Jason nonetheless.

Yield: 24 stacks

1 pound very fresh mozzarella cheese

1½ cups sun-dried tomatoes packed in oil

½ small bunch parsley, stems discarded

1 tablespoons chopped walnuts

1 small clove garlic

1 tablespoons chopped shallots

¼ teaspoon fresh lemon juice

¼ teaspoon sea salt

1 to 2 tablespoons extra-virgin olive oil

1½- to 1¾-inch-diameter deep biscuit cutter

Miniature muffin papers

Cut mozzarella into ¼-inch slices. Cut out 36 circles using the biscuit cutter, reserving the smoothest and most attractive slices for the top layers.

Drain sun-dried tomatoes and purée in a food processor until smooth.

Place parsley, walnuts, garlic, shallot, lemon juice, salt, and oil in a food processor and pulse until smooth.

Using the biscuit cutter as a form, layer a slice of mozzarella, a layer of pesto, another slice of cheese, a layer of sun-dried tomato purée, then the last layer of mozzarella. Gently hold the stack in place with your fingers while lifting the cutter away, leaving an artful stack. With a sharp knife, cut stack in half and place each half on a small cupcake paper before serving. Repeat, after wiping the cutter clean, with remaining ingredients and garnish with a dab of tomato purée. Serve at room temperature.

These can be prepared a day in advance and kept covered in the refrigerator.

Modify

Any tapenade or spread can substitute for the sun-dried tomatoes and pesto. Or try a spicy salsa and guacamole.

Magnify

In an 8-inch square glass pan, layer fresh basil leaves for the bottom first layer. Double ingredients and add a thin layer of mozzarella over the basil, a layer of tomato purée, and another layer of mozzarella. Then, using a pastry bag, pipe decorative stripes of pesto on top. Cut into 6 squares and serve as an appetizer. Garnish the plate with a sprinkle of diced fresh tomato or green, red, and orange bell peppers.

Zucchini Spirals

These light swirls of zucchini stuffed with a walnut-cheese pesto are a delight to make and eat.

Yield: 24 spirals

⅔ cup toasted walnuts (page 131)

1 cup fresh parsley

1 cup fresh basil leaves

1 clove garlic

½ cup grated Asiago cheese (2 ounces), plus extra for garnish

2 medium zucchini or yellow squash

Decorative toothpicks

Preheat oven to 425°F. In a food processor, purée all ingredients except zucchini until smooth.

Using a vegetable peeler, slice ⅛-inch-thick strips from the zucchini, discarding the first strip (with the most skin). Arrange slices on a work surface and spread a heaping teaspoon of pesto onto each strip. Roll up strips and secure with a toothpick. Sprinkle with cheese and place on a baking sheet. (Rolls can be prepared a day in advance and kept covered in the refrigerator.) Bake for 5 minutes or until the cheese has melted.

Modify

Replace zucchini with blanched carrot, walnuts with bread crumbs or almonds, basil with spinach, and Asiago with Swiss cheese.

Magnify

Lay three strips end to end, slightly overlapping, and spread with filling. Roll up to create a large spiral. Bake for 8 to 10 minutes or until heated through. Garnish the plate with small tomatoes and basil. Serves 8.

Olé Canapés

All the classic Mexican ingredients on a crunchy slice of jicama. Easy and delicious, and a welcome break from nachos.

Yield: 30 canapés

1 large jicama (about 1½ pounds), peeled and sliced ½ inch thick

One 15-ounce can, rinsed and drained, cooked black beans (about 2 cups)

1 cup grated white Monterey Jack cheese (4 ounces)

¾ cup pitted chopped black olives

3 tablespoons finely chopped green scallion

¼ cup finely chopped fresh cilantro

2 tablespoons chopped jalapeño pepper (optional)

Red salsa, as garnish

Extra cilantro leaves and olive slices, as garnish

2-inch round cutter

Cut 30 rounds from the jicama slices. (The rounds can be cut in advance and stored in an airtight container for up to 3 days.) Combine remaining ingredients in a medium bowl. (This topping can be made a day in advance and kept covered in the refrigerator until ready to use. Bring to room temperature before serving.) Spoon onto rounds; a kitchen teaspoon works best. Spoon a bit of salsa on top and garnish with a slice of olive and a cilantro leaf.

Modify

Replace black beans with garbanzo beans, cilantro with parsley, cheese with shredded dark chicken meat, and omit jalapeño. Serve on rounds cut from slices of Asian pear.

Magnify

Double recipe and fill 4 hollowed and blanched bell peppers. Omit jicama slices; 1 cup chopped jicama may be added to the filling. Makes 4 colorful light meals or starters that require no preheating.

Cheddar Shortbread with Pear Kumquat Salsa (page 104)

Pastry-Based Bites

Pastry that surrounds a tasty morsel is like pretty gift wrap around a wonderful present. The pastry in this collection includes a variety of pastry techniques borrowed from the dessert world, just applied to savory interiors—all with stunning results.

Don't let the word pastry intimidate you. Follow these easy instructions and impress your guests instead.

- Curried Tuna Triangles
- Cheddar Shortbread with Pear Kumquat Salsa
- Orange Pecan Brie Cups
- Scallion Puff Pillows
- Tart Cherry Chicken Puffs
- Wild Mushroom Rugelach
- Peach Asiago Crêpe Cones

Curried Tuna Triangles

Mrs. Muller, a good friend of my mother's, was a much more adventurous cook. It was she who gave us the recipe for curried tuna. Back then, anything curry was exotic and we couldn't get enough of this simple dish. When visiting my brother thirty years later, I asked what he would like for dinner. His answer: curried tuna. After all those years, we both still loved it. This filling, jazzed up just a bit, is an homage to Mrs. Muller and our favorite comfort food.

Yield: 24 triangles

1 tablespoon unsalted butter

1 tablespoon flour

1 teaspoon Worcestershire sauce

½ teaspoon sweet paprika

4 drops Tabasco sauce

½ cup whole milk

1 medium tomato, seeded and finely chopped

Two 6-ounce cans drained, flaked cooked tuna

1 tablespoon minced chives

1 tablespoon curry powder

8 sheets phyllo dough

8 tablespoons (1 stick) unsalted butter, melted

Chives and diced, seeded tomato, as garnish

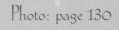

Photo: page 130

Melt 1 tablespoon butter in a small saucepan over medium heat. Add flour, Worcestershire, paprika, and Tabasco and whisk until it becomes a smooth roux. Slowly add milk, whisking to keep sauce smooth. Continue to cook over medium heat until sauce thickens, about 5 minutes, stirring occasionally. Add tomato, tuna, chives, and curry powder and cook for 2 minutes longer.

Preheat oven to 350°F. Line baking sheets with parchment paper. Lay out phyllo and cover with plastic wrap and a dampened towel to keep it from drying out. Remove 1 sheet and brush liberally with melted butter. Cut the sheet into 3 equal strips, each about 2¾ × 13 inches. Place a rounded teaspoon of filling on the lower right corner of 1 strip, then, as one would fold a flag (see diagram), fold phyllo corner to corner, creating a triangle encasing the filling. Repeat with remaining phyllo and filling. (Triangles can be frozen, unbaked, for up to a month. No need to defrost before baking.)

Place triangles on baking sheets 1 inch apart. Bake for 12 minutes or until golden brown.

Modify

Replace tuna with chopped cooked chicken, beef, or pork.

Magnify

Triple all ingredients except tuna and tomato and serve over rice. Makes 6 small plates.

Cheddar Shortbread with Pear Kumquat Salsa

The idea of a savory shortbread sandwich at first sounded like buttery overkill, but once I started to test this pairing of flaky, flavorful shortbread with the tart/sweet filling, I knew I had a very different flavor combination that would please my guests—and yours, I hope!

Yield: 16 sandwiches

2 cups finely grated white Cheddar cheese (about 8 ounces)

8 tablespoons (1 stick) unsalted butter, softened

1½ cups flour

¼ teaspoon salt

¼ teaspoon freshly ground pepper

Sea salt (or table salt)

2 large pears, preferably Comice, cored and chopped

2 small green scallions, finely chopped

2 teaspoons fresh lemon juice

2 tablespoons brown sugar

1 cup finely chopped seeded kumquats

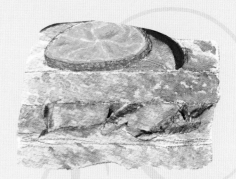

Photo: page 100

Preheat oven to 350°F. Combine cheese, butter, flour, ¼ teaspoon salt, and pepper in a large bowl. Beat until dough holds together. You may need to knead it briefly to ensure it is completely combined. Divide evenly in half.

Line an 8-inch square baking pan with plastic wrap and, using it as a mold, press half the dough into the bottom of the pan in an even layer. Invert dough onto a baking sheet, remove plastic wrap, and repeat with the second piece of dough. Refrigerate dough on baking sheets for 30 minutes.

Cut each square into sixteen 1 × 4-inch rectangles. Do not separate the rectangles. Sprinkle with salt and bake each scored sheet for 20 to 25 minutes or until lightly browned. Cut through rectangles again while the shortbread is still warm. (Shortbread can be stored in a cool place in an airtight container for up to 2 days or in the freezer for 2 months.)

Stir remaining ingredients together in a medium bowl. Create "sandwiches" with a thin layer of salsa between two shortbreads and a dollop of leftover salsa on top for garnish.

Modify

Replace kumquats with cranberries and some chopped walnuts.

Magnify

Use shortbread dough to line an 8- to 10-inch tart pan. Prebake crust until browned, about 20 minutes. Layer with unpeeled pear slices. Finely slice or chop kumquats; combine with scallions, lemon juice, and sugar, and spread evenly over pears. Combine 2 eggs with ½ cup milk and pour carefully to fill the crevices but not cover pear slices completely. Bake for 40 to 50 minutes at 375°F or until the filling is browned and set. Cut into 6 slices for a savory pastry first course.

Orange Pecan Brie Cups

I've come to one conclusion after years of serving hor d'oeuvres: Brie is the number one appetizer cheese. I've seen people swoon when you just mention the word. These little cups are long on orange tang, and with the creamy Brie and the crunch of pecans added, get out the smelling salts.

Yield: 24 cups

1 cup flour

¼ cup finely chopped pecans

½ teaspoon salt

⅛ teaspoon pepper

2 tablespoons unsalted butter, cold

¼ cup fresh orange juice, cold

8 ounces Brie, cold

2 tablespoons finely chopped orange zest

1 tablespoon fresh orange juice

1 teaspoon grated lemon zest

2 teaspoons fresh lemon juice

1 small red onion, finely chopped

4 teaspoons brown sugar

½ cup chopped pecans

Orange segments, as garnish

Miniature muffin pans

2½-inch round cutter

Preheat oven to 350°F. Brush muffin pan cups with butter. Combine flour, finely chopped pecans, salt, and pepper in a medium bowl. Cut butter into flour until the texture resembles cornmeal. Add ¼ cup orange juice and toss with a fork to distribute the moisture throughout. Gently press and knead dough just until it comes together. Divide dough into 2 pieces and shape into discs. Wrap in plastic wrap and refrigerate for at least 30 minutes.

Roll out 1 piece of dough on a floured surface to ⅛ inch thickness. Cut out 12 rounds and gently and evenly press them into muffin pans to form cups with edges level with the edge of the pan. Repeat with the remaining dough to create another 12 cups. Bake for 10 to 12 minutes until the

Continued on next page

Modify

For a tangy alternative, replace pecans in dough with chives, orange zest with 3 tablespoons chopped pear, orange and lemon juice with 5 teaspoons lemon juice, red onion with ¼ cup finely chopped scallions, and chopped pecans with chopped dried cranberries.

Magnify

Instead of the pastry cups, use puff pastry dough. Increase the size of the Brie round to almost a pound. Remove rind if desired and place the whole Brie in the center of the thawed sheet of puff pastry dough. Double remaining ingredients and spread on top. Gather puff pastry up and around the Brie, pinching it in the center. Brush with egg wash (see page 133) and bake at 400°F until the dough is puffed and golden brown. Serve hot, cutting a wedge for each guest.

dough is firm and just slightly browned. Cool. These can be prepared a week in advance and kept in a cool, dry container until ready to use.

Trim rind from Brie if you wish and cut into ¼-inch cubes. Keep refrigerated until ready to use.

Preheat oven to 350°F. Combine remaining ingredients in a small bowl. Add Brie cubes and toss until coated completely. Spoon equally into each pastry cup and place on a baking sheet. Just before serving, heat the cups just until the Brie becomes soft, about 3 to 5 minutes. Garnish with an orange segment before serving.

Wild Mushroom Rugelach (page 114)

Scallion Puff Pillows

Keep it simple. Elegant and easy, pastry and pine nuts need no fancy retinue.

Yield: 48 pillows

1 sheet puff pastry

Egg wash (see page 133)

15 scallions, green parts only, cut into 3-inch strips

2 tablespoons extra-virgin olive oil

¾ cup finely diced yellow bell pepper

1 cup toasted pine nuts (see page 131)

Photo: pages 6 and 101

Preheat oven to 375°F. Line a baking sheet with parchment. Measure pastry sheet; if necessary, roll out to a 9 × 12-inch rectangle. Cut puff pastry sheet into forty-eight 1½-inch squares. With a pastry brush, brush each square on top with egg wash and place on baking sheet, 1 inch apart. Bake squares until puffed and lightly browned, about 15 minutes. Cool. (Pastry squares, if kept in an airtight container, can be made up to a week in advance.)

Heat oil until very hot in a medium skillet over medium-high heat. Sauté scallions until they are wilted, about 3 to 5 minutes. Add yellow pepper and pine nuts; stir to combine and heat through for 30 seconds. Top each puff pastry square with a tablespoon of scallion topping. Don't hesitate to flatten the top to create a level surface; the broken pastry will be hidden by the topping.

Modify

Replace scallions with 2 cups thin spinach strips, and pine nuts with finely chopped toasted walnuts. Tasty!

Magnify

Use 1½ cups of your choice of sautéed chopped vegetables instead of scallions and nuts. Cut puff pastry into 3 × 4-inch rectangles. Brush with egg wash (see page 133) and bake for 20 to 25 minutes until golden brown. Spread a piece of baked pastry with a thin layer of vegetables, top with more pastry, add another layer of vegetables, and finish with a final pastry layer. Repeat with remaining pastry and filling. Serve with garnish to start your next fancy dinner.

Tart Cherry Chicken Puffs

One of the most popular finger sandwich fillings I've served for an afternoon tea is a mixture of smoked turkey with a variety of dried fruits, almonds, and spices. These little cream puffs deliver a chicken variation that is easy and irresistible.

Yield: 24 puffs

4 tablespoons (½ stick) unsalted butter

⅛ teaspoon salt

½ cup flour

2 eggs

8 ounces smoked chicken

¾ cup tart dried cherries

1 cup toasted walnuts (see page 131)

1 tablespoon fresh lemon juice

1½ teaspoons dried juniper berries

2 ounces cream cheese, softened

½ cup plain yogurt

3 scallions, chopped, both green and white parts

½ teaspoon salt

Freshly ground pepper, to taste

Combine ½ cup water and butter in a small saucepan and bring to a boil over high heat. Add salt and flour all at once and cook, stirring constantly, until dough pulls away from the sides of the pan and forms a ball. Remove from heat and add eggs one at a time, beating well after each addition. The dough will be very smooth. Refrigerate for 30 minutes.

Preheat oven to 400°F. Line baking sheets with parchment paper. Place dough by the teaspoonful, mounding as high as you can, on the baking sheet, 1½ inches apart. Bake for 15 to 18 minutes until brown and hollow (tap with a spoon). Cool. Puffs can be baked up to a week in advance and kept in an airtight container until ready to use.

Grind juniper berries with a mortar and pestle, or in a clean coffee mill. Pulse remaining ingredients in a food processor until chopped and combined but not puréed. (Filling can be made a few days in advance and kept in the refrigerator until ready to assemble.)

Cut the tops off puffs, fill, replace tops, and serve.

Modify

Replace chicken with 10 ounces smoked salmon, omit cherries and walnuts, and add ¼ cup fresh dill.

Magnify

Add ½ cup finely chopped parsley to the puff dough before baking. Do not put filling through food processor; instead, cut chicken into large chunks. Add a few tablespoons of milk and combine into a chicken salad that can be served in 4 radicchio cups, with puffs served on the side as a garnish.

Wild Mushroom Rugelach

For years I've been making classic sweet rugelach for winter holidays. When my friend Alan gave me a large supply of wild mushrooms, I was thinking about unusual ways I could use this delicious gift. Then it hit me! A savory rugelach. The tart, flaky dough pairs well with non-dessert ingredients. Use your favorite type of mushroom or mix several varieties together. You'll be wild about them, too.

Yield: 24 to 30 rugelach

⅔ cup flour

⅛ teaspoon salt

⅛ teaspoon baking powder

2 ounces cream cheese, softened

4 tablespoons (½ stick) unsalted butter, softened

1 egg yolk

1½ teaspoons sour cream

1 teaspoon vanilla extract

1 tablespoon unsalted butter

½ cup finely chopped shallots

1½ cups mushrooms, finely chopped

⅔ cup sweet Italian sausage

1 teaspoon fresh chopped rosemary or ½ teaspoon dried

Photo: page 109

Whisk flour, salt, and baking powder together in a medium bowl. In another bowl, using a hand mixer, beat cream cheese and softened butter until light, about 2 minutes. Add egg yolk, sour cream, and vanilla and beat at medium speed until smooth. At low speed, add dry ingredients and mix just until combined. Divide dough into 2 pieces and wrap each in plastic wrap. Refrigerate for a minimum of 3 hours or up to overnight.

Melt 1 tablespoon butter in a skillet over medium heat, and sauté shallots until translucent and tender, about 2 minutes. Remove half and set aside. Add mushrooms, sausage, and rosemary. Cook until sausage is cooked through and moisture from the mushrooms has evaporated, about 3 to 5 minutes. Set aside to cool.

Preheat oven to 325°F. Roll half of the cold pastry dough out onto a floured surface ⅛ inch thick to create a 6 × 14-inch rectangle. Sprinkle half of the mushroom/sausage filling over the surface and roll up the long end, jelly-roll style, to create a 14-inch roll. If dough has become too soft, refrigerate it until it holds its shape. Cut roll into fourteen 1-inch pieces. Repeat with remaining dough and filling. Place rugelach seam side down on a parchment-lined baking sheet 2 inches apart. Sprinkle reserved shallots on top. Bake for 35 to 40 minutes until golden brown.

Modify

Omit mushrooms; spread garlic butter lightly over the dough and sprinkle with assorted fresh herbs, shallots, and sunflower seeds as a tasty meatless variation.

Magnify

Double ingredients. Roll the dough out ¼ inch thick and cut into 4-inch circles. Spoon filling onto one side of each pastry disc, fold over, and press edges down with a fork to make mushroom/ sausage pastries. Serve 2 per person for lunch or as a meal starter. Serves 4.

Peach Asiago Crêpe Cones

Every time I eat a crêpe I think of my first trip to Paris, eating huge crêpes from the street stands. That rich batter makes for an excellent hors d'oeuvre container, and these little cones, served warm and nutty with the distinctive flavor of Asiago cheese, are sure to please.

Yield: 18 to 20 cones

8 ounces Asiago cheese

1 cup peach marmalade

¼ cup brown sugar, packed

⅔ cup toasted, chopped pecans (see page 131)

7 or 8 crêpes (see pages 66–67)

2½-inch round cutter

18 to 20 small fresh rosemary sprigs, as garnish

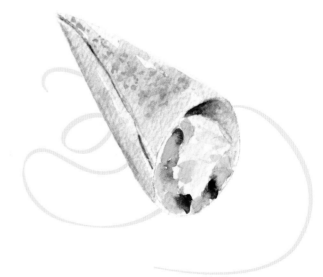

Preheat oven to 350°F. Line a baking sheet with parchment paper. Cut Asiago into ½-inch cubes. Combine cubes, marmalade, brown sugar, and pecans in a medium bowl.

Cut three 2½-inch rounds from each crêpe. Curl each round into a cone and use a rosemary sprig as a toothpick to keep the cone closed. Spoon a scant tablespoon of filling into each cone. Place on the baking sheet and heat for 3 to 5 minutes or until the Asiago is warm and soft but not melted. These are best served while warm. Cones can be assembled and filled in advance and kept in the refrigerator for up to 3 days.

Modify

Replace marmalade and pecans with 1 tablespoon minced fresh thyme and 1 teaspoon lemon zest.

Magnify

Double the filling. Keep crêpes whole. Spoon filling in an even line down the center of each crêpe, then roll them up, place in a baking dish, and heat at 350°F until the centers are soft and gooey, about 5 minutes. Garnish with fresh peach slices and a sprinkle of chopped pecans to finish off this pleasing first course.

Assorted Naked Canapés: Sesame Crisps (page 120); Bacon Biscuits (page 122); and Citrus Crackers (page 126)

Naked Canapés

Sometimes you just need a snack. These savory crackers can all be prepared in advance, ready for delivering leftovers with panache to anyone dropping in unexpectedly or for your own midnight cravings.

- Sesame Crisps
- Bacon Biscuits
- Pecan Mounds
- Cornmeal Scones
- Citrus Crackers
- Thyme Diamond Wafers

Sesame Crisps

The first version of my book Dessert Canapés *included a sesame taco with mango filling. This recipe never made it into the finished book, but I could never let go of the taste of the sesame crisp; it was that good. I knew I would use the recipe sometime, and here it is, only in a savory version.*

Yield: 20 crisps

2 tablespoons corn syrup

1 teaspoon red miso paste*

1 teaspoon ground ginger

4 drops sesame oil

2 tablespoons flour

4 tablespoons (½ stick) unsalted butter, softened

2 tablespoons sugar

1 cup sesame seeds, half black* and half white

Photo: pages 45, 46, and 118

Preheat oven to 400°F. Line a baking sheet with a silicone sheet or parchment paper. Combine all the ingredients in a small bowl and mix using a rubber spatula until batter is smooth and free from lumps.

Drop batter, 1 heaping teaspoon (measuring spoon) per crisp, 2 inches apart on baking sheet. Bake for 5 minutes. Cool completely for flat crisps. For cups, set aside to rest for 1 to 2 minutes, just long enough so you can pick them up without burning your hands. Press them into muffin pans to shape into cups. If crisps firm up too much to form, pop them back in the oven for 30 seconds. Place cooled crisps between layers of waxed paper to prevent breakage when storing at room temperature.

*Black sesame seeds and miso paste are available in the Asian foods section of some grocery stores or at Asian specialty markets. If you cannot find red miso, light miso can be substituted.

Bacon Biscuits

Bacon is appearing in everything these days, even chocolate, desserts, and ice cream. It's trendy today, but the Germans have been using bacon in savory biscuits for centuries. This flaky biscuit, adapted from a German recipe, is as great alone as with other ingredients.

Yield: 20 biscuits

½ pound bacon, sliced

14 tablespoons (1¾ sticks) unsalted butter, softened

⅓ cup heavy cream

2 cups flour

2-inch biscuit cutter

Photo: page 118

Fry bacon in a large skillet over medium heat until crisp. Place on paper towels to drain. Reserve 2 tablespoons of bacon grease in a bowl and set aside to cool and harden. Discard or reserve remaining grease for another use. Crumble bacon.

Mix together all ingredients including reserved bacon grease in a medium bowl using a rubber spatula or hand mixer. Divide dough into thirds, wrap well, and refrigerate for 1 hour or until firm.

Preheat oven to 375°F. Line 2 baking sheets with parchment paper. Take one-third of the dough from the refrigerator and roll out on a lightly floured surface ⅛ inch thick. Cut rounds from dough with the cutter and prick each round with a fork a few times. Repeat with remaining dough. Bake for 10 minutes or until bottoms and edges are lightly browned. Cool.

Pecan Mounds

Here's a perfectly crunchy something for those who love nuts or don't tolerate wheat. You may have had spicy nuts before, but these mounds take ground pecans to a new level. In an airtight container, they'll last a very long time.

Yield: 20 mounds

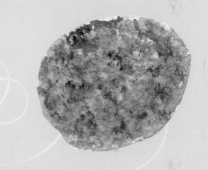

1½ cups pecans

¼ cup egg whites (2 large egg whites)

1 tablespoon unsalted butter, softened

⅛ teaspoon cayenne pepper

Preheat oven to 350°F. Line 2 baking sheets with parchment paper. Grind pecans in a food processor or spice grinder to generate 1 cup of ground nuts. *Don't overprocess:* you want ground pecans, not pecan butter.

Combine all ingredients in a medium bowl, with a rubber spatula to create a smooth batter. Mound a kitchen teaspoonful onto baking sheets 1 to 2 inches apart (they will spread a bit). Bake for 10 minutes. Cool to firm up before removing.

Cornmeal Scones

People forget how delicious properly made scones can taste. The "hockey pucks" sold today are a far cry from the delicate bread that once was associated only with afternoon tea. With these, there is no need to add butter or filling. Just a mug of tea and a moment to relax and savor being alive.

Yield: 20 small scones

1 cup flour

¾ cup yellow cornmeal

2 tablespoons sugar

2½ teaspoons baking powder

½ teaspoon baking soda

¾ teaspoon salt

8 tablespoons (1 stick) unsalted butter, cold

1 cup corn kernels, fresh or frozen (optional)

1 egg

¾ cup buttermilk

Egg wash (page 133)

1-inch biscuit cutter

Preheat oven to 425°F. Line 2 baking sheets with parchment paper. Place dry ingredients in a food processor and pulse a few times to blend. Add butter in tablespoon-sized pieces and pulse just enough to create the consistency of coarse meal. Add corn if desired and pulse a few times. Transfer to a large bowl. Whisk egg and buttermilk together in a small bowl and add to dry ingredients. Mix just until dough is evenly moistened. Turn onto a lightly floured surface and knead gently until just combined.

Pat dough out 1 inch thick. Cut out 1-inch rounds and place on baking sheets 1 to 2 inches apart. Brush tops with egg wash and bake for 10 minutes or until scones are golden brown and firm.

Citrus Crackers

The words "citrus" and "cracker" together immediately evoke a sweet something, but this is no dessert! The minimal touch of sugar and sprinkling of kosher salt enhance the orange and lemon flavors, producing a savory citrus delight.

Yield: 32 crackers

1 egg

1 tablespoon fresh orange juice

2 teaspoons fresh lemon juice

1½ cups flour

¼ cup sugar

½ teaspoon salt

½ teaspoon baking powder

8 tablespoons (1 stick) unsalted butter, frozen

1 tablespoon finely grated orange zest

2 teaspoons finely grated lemon zest

Kosher salt

2-inch round or football-shaped cutter

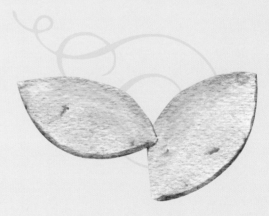

Photo: page 118

Preheat oven to 350°F. Line 2 baking sheets with parchment paper. Whisk egg and orange and lemon juices together in a small bowl. In a medium bowl, combine flour, sugar, salt, and baking powder. Using the large holes on a box grater, grate frozen butter into dry ingredients. Rub butter into flour with your fingertips until the texture is like coarse meal. Stir in grated zests. Add egg-juice mixture and combine until moist clumps form. Turn dough out onto a floured surface and knead gently until dough comes together.

Roll out ¼ inch thick, cut out shapes, and arrange on baking sheets. Sprinkle lightly with kosher salt and bake until firm, about 15 minutes.

Thyme Diamond Wafers

There is something very special and challenging about making something that we generally take for granted. People eat crackers out of the box and give little thought to how they are made, let alone how much better they are when homemade. Food, even a simple cracker, tastes better whenever one participates in the process.

Yield: 48 wafers

2 cups flour

3 tablespoons chopped fresh thyme or 1 tablespoon dried

1½ teaspoons salt

1 teaspoon sugar

3 tablespoons unsalted butter, cold

1 cup heavy cream

1 egg white, lightly beaten

Kosher salt

Chopped fresh thyme, as garnish

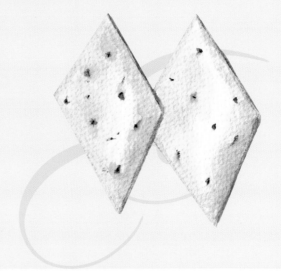

Preheat oven to 375°F. Combine flour, thyme, 1½ teaspoons salt, and sugar in a food processor by pulsing a few times. Cut butter into pieces and add. Pulse until butter is in pea-sized pieces. Then, while running machine briefly, add cream. Process just until dough forms. Divide into 4 pieces, wrap in plastic wrap, and refrigerate for about 30 minutes until firm.

Cut a piece of parchment paper to fit baking sheet. Roll out 1 piece of dough at a time on parchment paper into a ⅛ inch-thick rectangle and place on baking sheet. Score dough into 4 × 2-inch diamonds. Brush with egg white and sprinkle with salt. Garnish with a sprinkling of thyme. Repeat with remaining dough.

Bake until golden brown and crisp, 15 to 20 minutes. When completely cool, break into individual crackers.

Rose Beef Canapés (page 34); Broccoli Soufflés (page 78); Curried Tuna Triangles (page 102)

Helpful Tips

Toasting Nuts

Place any nut (except for pine nuts) on a baking sheet and place in an oven preheated to 350°F. Stir the nuts occasionally. Most nuts will take about 10 minutes to toast. You can usually tell when they're done from their aroma, but be careful: nuts can burn easily.

Pine nuts are especially delicate.
Toast them in a frying pan over
medium heat; you must stir
the nuts frequently to prevent
scorching.

Blanching Vegetables

Wash, drain, sort, trim, and cut vegetables to size.

Drop vegetables into 4 quarts of boiling water for the appropriate time (see below) and then remove. Do not mix vegetables that have different cooking times.

After removing vegetables from boiling water, immediately drop into ice water to stop cooking. Drain thoroughly before using.

Vegetable	Blanching time (in minutes)
Asparagus, medium stalk	3
String or wax beans	3
Broccoli, 1½-inch florets	3
Carrots, sliced or in strips	2
Cauliflower, 1-inch florets	3
Celery sticks	3
Sweet peas in the pod	1½ to 2½
Bell pepper strips or rings	2

Egg Wash

Whisk together 1 egg with 1 tablespoon water in a small bowl. Brush on pastry before baking to add a glossy sheen and aid in browning.

Estimating Hors d'Oeuvre Quantities

If the gathering lasts for 1 to 1½ hours followed by dinner, you will need 6 or 7 small bites per person.

If the gathering is early, right after office hours, and people are hungry, you will need 10 to 12 small bites per person.

If the gathering starts about 6:00 p.m. and is not followed by dinner, you will need a minimum of 14 to 16 small bites per person.

If the gathering is 4 hours long, regardless of starting time, you will need 12 small bites per person.

If it is a wedding reception from 2:30 to 5:30, you will need 8 small bites per person.

For all other occasions, estimate 4 small bites per person per hour for the first 2 hours and 2 small bites per person for every hour after.

This is based on a served gathering, but if your gathering is self-serve, you need to know your crowd and may need to prepare more!

Ideas to Enhance Your Next Entertaining Experience

Balance the selection.

Vary your menu to include meat, seafood, and vegetable hors d'oeuvres. It is wise to include one or two very dramatic savories in the mix for immediate eye appeal (remember—people eat with their eyes first!), and as long as the flavor of the entire menu is a pleasurable experience, your guests will remember your event with joy.

Know your budget.

Another reason to vary the selection is to keep your costs under control. Seafood and some meats cost more than pastry-based or vegetable savories, so dazzle your guests with one expensive bite and widen the menu to include other lower-cost recipes. You can also save money by using a server instead of placing the dishes of hors d'oeuvres on a table. A server can control how much food is offered to the crowd at a time and will also make sure your guests never see a "picked over" serving dish. If you pace the serving appropriately, your guests will never notice they're being "rationed."

Manage your time.

Some hors d'oeuvres take longer to prepare than others, and some can be made entirely in advance, while others may be made only partially in advance. Don't get stuck in the kitchen with several last-minute dishes while your guests are wondering where you are.

Know your audience.

Foods on the cutting edge of culinary style may not suit a "mac 'n' cheese" crowd. Choose appropriately. If you know of dietary restrictions for even one guest, it is wise to include at least one hors d'oeuvre that meets his or her requirements.

Don't give your crowd too much choice.

A limited but varied selection will encourage your guests to nibble and mingle, not wait for something better.

Avoid food that takes too long to eat or otherwise distracts from the event's purpose.

If you are preparing for a cocktail party, keep the savories to one or two bites each and make them easy to pick up so that people can mingle rather than have to sit or juggle silverware in order to eat. A bite in the hand is worth two on the plate! If you are serving an afternoon tea, make the portions small in keeping with the Victorian tradition of variety. If your small bites are the starter for a sit-down meal, remember that this is just the beginning; there will be plenty more later.

Choose hors d'oeuvres that will delight your guests, not frustrate them.

Hors d'oeuvres must look fresh, with interesting shapes, designs, and colors: not soggy and never smelly. Choose savories with recognizable ingredients or else make sure your server can communicate how each bite is prepared and entice the crowd to try something new. Always have a place close by for depositing toothpicks, seafood or nut shells, or inedible garnishes. Always have small napkins close at hand.

Enjoy your guests!

Asian Beef Carpaccio (page 46)

Resources

Atlantic Spice Company
North Truro, MA
800-316-7965
www.atlanticspice.com
Wide assortment of cooking spices.

Ateco
Glen Cove, NY
800-645-7170
www.atecousa.com
Pastry bags, pastry tips, Silpats, cutters.

The Baker's Store Catalog
Norwich, VT
800-827-6836
www.kingarthurflour.com
Specialty foods, chocolate, cookie cutters, and more.

The Chefs' Warehouse
Bronx, NY
718-842-8700
www.ChefsWarehouse.com
Source for high-end pastry ingredients and equipment.

Frontier Natural Products Co-op
Norway, IA
800-669-3275
www.FrontierCoop.com
Organic herbs and natural kitchen supplies.

JB Prince
New York, NY
800-473-0577
www.jbprince.com
Professional-grade bakeware and equipment.

La Cuisine
Alexandria, VA
800-521-1176
www.lacuisineus.com
General equipment for cooking and baking and a wide assortment of cookie cutters.

Mierco Inc.
Port Townsend, WA
888-277-8838
www.mierco.com
Fine European linens pictured on pages 25, 34, and 74.

N. Y. Cake
New York, NY
877-NYCAKE-8
www.nycake.com
General bakeware and cookie cutters.

Penzeys Spices
Muskego, WI
800-741-7787
www.penzeys.com
Great source for spices and herbs.

Scandicrafts Cuisine Internationale
Camarillo, CA
800-966-5489
www.scandicrafts.com
Silicone molds, bakeware, and baking utensils.

REVOL USA
Cumming, GA
678-456-8671
Elisabeth Cairo, info@revol-usa.com
www.revol-usa.com
Delicate but strong dishware for elegant presentation. Revol dishware is pictured on the cover and pages 45, 67, 74, and 87.

Sur la Table
Seattle, WA
800-243-0852
www.surlatable.com
Decorative baking equipment, cookie cutters, utensils, and more.

Williams-Sonoma
San Francisco, CA
877-812-6235
www.williams-sonoma.com
Baking equipment, specialty foods, cookie cutters, and more.

Wilton Industries
Woodridge, IL
800-794-5866
www.wilton.com
Cookie cutters, pastry bags, tips, and assorted bakeware.